A Sibling Within

A Sibling Within

J. K. Remel

ISBN: 978-1-4269-3743-9 (sc)

Trafford rev.12/22/2010

www.trafford.com

North America & International
toll-free: 1 888 232 4444 (USA & Canada)
phone: 250 383 6864 ♦ fax: 812 355 4082

For Doris, my sibling within.

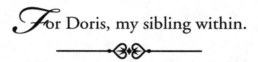

Chapter 1

Each of us has one. I find three without searching my room begins a speech I gave in college. I meant a calendar back then. Today, perhaps it's more about books - the book inside us which holds our story. Or more apt, theirs told through us.

"The things we tell strangers!" gasps the woman next to me. My daughter Madeline has just learned to swim. We are on vacation in town for my parent's sixtieth wedding anniversary. It's the Vermont indoor pool for Madeline.

We remember things we do for the very first time, even those we do for the last. We remember where we were, who we were with and those who are no longer with us.

The woman in front of me in the hotel breakfast line laments she misses her sister. Guilty, not so much she missed her older sibling, rather she wishes she was still around to shoulder some of the responsibility of caring for their disabled younger sister.

I tell her my older daughter finally learned how to swim. Abby already knew, learning years before in Phoenix. The things we tell strangers. Suppose that is the essence of books, we tell strangers what happens, remind ourselves what happened, and maybe even tell our own story unbeknownst to us at the time. Thus the sometimes awkward gasp, "Oh, the things we tell strangers!"

Other times we are stopped in our tracks by a story. Either the day to day presents some physical reminder we hope to never see again much less experience those sensations lodged in our body, perhaps muscle memory. Other times a book recommended to us does much the same.

Not so much the things we tell strangers, rather strangers telling us too familiar things. It hits home. It resonates. It's as though we read of our own story, even through pages thirty to fifty those twenty pages which define lives.

This morning I call an older sister to wish her a happy birthday. She turns fifty two and says we aren't kids anymore. I tell her I'd seen my books at Goodwill. I donated fifty books two weeks ago and there they were on the shelves. I knew they were mine as I always write in the date and zip code on the second page.

I spot one, telling the person next to me it is a book I'd recently dropped off. Then I see a second one. I smile thinking how cool to see my books on the shelves. Not books I'd written, rather those I recently read and circulated via Goodwill. I show the person next to me my numbers on page two to prove they once were in my hands. "Did they work?" she asks.

Later I spot yet a third one. It made me realize how exciting it would be to someday have our books on store shelves, our books the ones we write. The ones with the things we tell strangers. I share with my sister next in line in age I brought home a Starbucks coffee and found a book on that company while at Goodwill. *Starbucked*, all you want to know about the Seattle coffee roaster.

I mention a recent bestseller someone recommended. The narrative is dark and I later asked the person who recommended it just what was it about this particular book, what "worked" if you will? My older sister says "Oh, I read that one. I loved it. I even sent a copy to mom and dad." We are on speaker phone. The birthday greeting is sung, now the kids laugh out loud, knowing I'm not a fan of that best selling book.

Books, the things we tell strangers, affect each of us differently. We hear what the author writes depending on our own life experience. My sister next in line younger than me left two days after her fifth birthday. Maybe the recent bestseller went too close there and most times I prefer to stay away from there.

Each of us has one, or maybe three. We have our family, friends and work life. Writers have another life which takes on a life of its own. We travel through words, even those words, the things we tell strangers. Then there are times we are pulled away by those who've left long ago. Some days it is a physical reminder along our walking path, other times a book which falls in our lap.

They echo long afterwards, they too write our books. We in essence use their words to tell a story to strangers. Sometimes their words tell our story regardless if we realize it ahead of time. Those who've left are often still by our side.

The kids laugh out loud. I pause, thinking perhaps my parents would not care to relive details still painful thirty five years later. A load of logs crushed my younger sister. Those are my book's details; still the bestseller went close enough for me to relive some painful memories. Books do this, somewhere buried within the things we tell strangers, we move them. Often, we as authors can't know in advance how our words will be received.

Sometimes we aren't even aware we tell our story, until we gasp and maybe regret we shared our words, how they are spoken, or even guilty for thinking much less saying out loud how we feel. Still few lives are full without a combination of family, friends and work, our writing and those who live, write and travel beside us each day going forward. We take them along, maybe they take us along - a sibling within.

Chapter 2

Each of us has one, a story or three. We tell them we are working on it, knowing getting our words to the page is the least of it. Our book has already been written, now we must get through the words. Varied as the details may be, they make us who we are, and write our books. Rather than a notation on a calendar, they fill our books and tell our story one setting at a time. How we frame our story differentiates our writing, where we place the reader, the setting.

Tonight while walking through our neighborhood, a modern subdivision with similar homes and varied landscapes, I see a truck - a late 1960's Ford.

The red Ford.

The white grill.

The load of wood.

All that's missing is my sister with the oversized yellow polka-dotted hat and her five year old hand waving. She did this years ago in most everyone's bucolic Vermont.

I later return to take its picture. Now Abby asks about the truck as she looks through her digital camera photographs. Why did I take that picture?

It stopped me in my tracks on a walk around our neighborhood. It would work as the front cover to my book. It finally wrote the book I've shelved for too long. I complete three others and start more, yet this one resonates most with me. Maybe like Michener's fourth effort, mine too will be widely read.

Still we write for an audience of one, we write for ourselves. Setting pulls us in and only later does the storyline take over. It's been thirty five years since middle school and the big red truck delivered its load of logs.

Earlier I had spent a week or two at my cousins' house when my sister was born. I remember being disappointed when told she had been born days before. Why was I still at their house? Today I wonder why the rush to return to our overcrowded family situation. I find three without searching my room could have meant siblings back then.

Suppose we are most familiar with what we know the setting which later writes our books, the things we later tell strangers. While my cousin was dating, her soon to be husband asks, "What do you plan to do with your life?" She interrupts him saying I am just a kid, even adults aren't always sure where their lives will lead, what they will hear as their life progresses so to speak.

Chapter 3

We write about it so others can read along and ideally hear more of their own story; the one which echoes their voice, their life. Perhaps not necessarily the one they planned for themselves, much less recognize in someone else's words. Still books do this on occasion, the better ones do it every time. We read of ourselves blended within someone else's detail.

Stories move, stir, and at times stop us in our tracks. We read of ourselves, our life echoed in the detail, our voice echoed in the writing, words echoed in our story. Even those stories penciled in the early morning fog. The stories written long ago amid a Tenderloin hotel lobby. The stories left behind in a Vermont sawmill pond, or begun there.

Stories surround us. Once we have a certain number of character sketches the story is written, the story writes itself. All that's left is to shuffle the deck of characters and weave them into our writing.

That is the hard part, where does the story start or even end. Like all good stories they start in the middle. Inside the middle, start there and then return to introduce and later conclude what we have written. Some days it is that simple, we write what we've read; imagined or maybe lived which seems fiction at this point, foreign to us, foreign to our life today. Still we must add those characters and include ourselves in the mix to write our books.

Writing echoes our voice. We use details from our life to write our own story. Sometimes we use details from our life to write the story of others, the story of humanity reflected within those details. Even the twenty difficult pages which tell our story, the parts that uniquely define our lives. We write so others can read along and ideally hear more of their own story.

Each of us has one, a story filled with laughter, tears, activity and relationship. Each of us has one, a story or three.

We live in a typical neighborhood, half go broke, and the other half don't speak to each other, like family - extended and nuclear.

Life is serious and dire for many; still the residents within the early morning hotel lobby within the Tenderloin became family. While perhaps limited financially, they did talk among themselves. Just after midnight many lingered in the lobby to spend time with fellow residents in the subsidized housing just steps away from San Francisco's opulence.

Madeline runs into my den, "Timberline is featured on this week's episode of Secret Millionaire" she says. I finish inputting my second edit onto the computer. I finish writing more chapters in a book on my experience years ago as a night desk clerk. The main job requirement is keeping the front door locked after midnight. I input my edit revisions, adding a sentence or three.

I rethink the title as I write along. I want to capture the idea of family: family within our nuclear birth family, family within the Tenderloin, family within humanity. The family within each of our own experience.

I write another paragraph; Madeline interrupts with what is on television. I dismiss it as the excitement of writing a book overtakes the moment. Writing a book energizes, knowing it is a line we will go with gives it extra excitement. I close down the computer and put the second edit of my manuscript away. Later walking to the kitchen, my wife mentions the Secret Millionaire has a difficult time in the Tenderloin.

That makes more sense, why would they secretly spend time atop Mount Hood at Timberline Lodge. Not the place which comes to mind for people struggling, in need of charity, people in dire need of a sibling. I watch as the millionaire meets a few in the forgotten land amid San Francisco's splendor. I know the neighborhood well; I once worked there and literally just finished writing a few more chapters on the Tenderloin earlier - minutes earlier.

I watch as they feature a few of the Tenderloin residents. Some begin a new life; others bring hope to people who leave behind perilous situations. I watch as I reflect on the place which was part of my life years before, knowing not much changes in the neighborhood. It's not the San Francisco many envision when thinking of everyone's favorite city. It exists nonetheless, not just in San Francisco. There are figurative Tenderloins throughout our world, perhaps a corner away from our own neighborhoods.

We write about it, we feature it on television programs such as Secret Millionaire. Others are inside, in the middle, making a difference in someone else's life, being a sibling to someone. That's all any of us can hope to accomplish, whether with a check, a book, or actively engaging our lives in service to others. It matters to the sibling within each of us, being available to someone, even on the graveyard shift inside the middle of the Tenderloin.

This residential hotel group is indeed family, perhaps sibling to each other as they sort through their lives. We all do, reaching out to others as the business of life continues around the corner.

Stories surround us if we'll take the time to notice. We write knowing like the fog outside our ideas will flow, within our writing words begin to tell a story. A story sometimes is not readily available at the start. Still we continue, we take it sentence by sentence, character by character and ultimately one setting at a time. Sometimes it is a child's family banner which waves from across a grade school library, it simply reads, Sibling To: No One.

We write in the early morning, before the routine of life takes over. We hear the coffee pot beep, the kids pour cereal, the pop of their toasts. We listen in to the activity a room away, sometimes a hotel lobby room away. We listen to what is going on outside, reflect on what is happening inside and too often those settings which stop us.

Writing takes a break from routine, takes a break from life. It expresses what goes on in our lives. Some days we reflect on an activity we oversaw or participated in - even decades before.

We write during the same morning session in our den, which is the only part similar day to day. We write for several pages at a time, each day our story builds, twists, and finds its words.

Many expect to make major change in one leap. Life is a series of consecutive small steps, only later, often much later, do we come to realize the breadth of our leap. Gradually over time we write something, something important and relevant to us. Ideally others find it also timely - our words get read by them.

We write for an audience of one, only later are we willing to share our words, thoughts and experiences with others once those phrases have been edited to form exactly what we intend to say. Most times we stop just short of finishing. No story is told in its entirety; the story goes on, even those penciled in on paper, in early morning autumn fog.

I've considered writing a book on the residential hotel inside San Francisco's Tenderloin district for some time. Read once we have a certain number of character sketches the story is written. All we have left is to shuffle the deck of characters and weave them inside within our story.

Inside the middle, life is lived, inside the middle. Stories start in the middle, in the midst of family, in the midst of residential hotels, in the midst of our everyday life. Just as travel opens new opportunities, new vistas, so too for the people we meet. It's true whether we are the ones moving through foreign territory or new people passing through our neighborhood: a connection is made, a relationship builds, and a story is found.

Sometimes it is our privilege to enhance another's life. More often it is others who augment or contribute to our lives. The Tenderloin district within San Francisco is aptly named. Located in the heart of the city, many bypass this region on to elsewhere. We will meet a few locals within the ensuing pages.

I worked there and have never forgotten the experience, the place or the people met while on a graveyard shift keeping the front door locked. Sometimes it seemed I was keeping the residents safe, other times keeping the neighborhood safe from some of the residents. I vacuumed the lobby and received the nightly donut delivery while keeping this front door locked.

Each had their story, a lobby full of life stories. Many had once thrived and then due to health reasons they are left in subsidized housing. Others make not so wise personal choices along the way. Each morning many gather in the front lobby as I sit at the desk overlooking the group of residents. The donuts being eaten, and the vacuum back in storage. The piano quiet at my right. The front door key safely in my pocket.

Inside the middle I sit and overhear their everyday schedules, their future hopes, their pasts, their lives today. Each has a story, yet all of them are confined to this subsidized residential hotel amid the splendor of San Francisco. Incongruent, inside the middle. I often reflect on those times: the different jobs, the various locations, the people met in those jobs and locations - the Tenderloin included.

Chapter 4

————————⟨3◆E⟩————————

The day to day fills our pages and tells the story. We attend the party, and pet the new dog. We log in our lives, one day at a time. There is schedule within the everyday writing.

We write at our desks, at the birthday party, even as the new pet is introduced. We write long after the candles are blown out, the birthday candles atop a Baskin Robbins ice cream cake. The cake with the face of the new puppy atop. The cake with those candles which insist on relighting, all ten of them.

All of us watching have a story to log in, once home or still at the party. We write about our lives and the people who share our lives. We live our art which is the writing of words, the recording of moments. Sights, sounds, even birthday parties are reflected within our pages.

They add backdrop, or even tell the story. The scent, the smoke, the story, the lobby full of stories lived out in front of us. The things we tell strangers, the loss of loved ones who leave us abruptly, unannounced - other times we move on.

We each begin in different places. The in between, our everyday, our personal routines are written within. Life is lived out differently for each of us, still there is a common bond, and we connect throughout our day. So too with writing, it connects us to our experience. It connects us to our readers: our readers listen along, participate in the birthday party, and see behind the scenes to writing.

Setting sets the stage; the setting settles in the reader and initially captures the moment for the author. We choose the backdrop, the background music. The story fills in from setting, from the birthday party, from those candles having a hard time staying extinguished.

A story is much the same. It resurfaces until it is written. It won't go away until it is told. A plot much like those candles provides light and heat to a story, without them the story lacks warmth, connection.

It is simply words on a page, rather than an engaging story. All stories begin as mere words. Writers log in their words and only later in the rereading and editing process does a message present itself. It is the fun part of writing, writing reveals itself.

We trust our words have a story to tell. A story may be long in coming, yet the story eventually surfaces, sometimes decades later. Writing is exciting for the writer, we are the story's first reader. Only after a timely rereading, editing process are we ready to share our story with others.

Autumn is here, the colors change with each cold night. The rains occur more often. There is a change in the air. We write of routine and the changes around us, as we focus on the moment at hand. We notice the shadow of our hand on the page, only later do we see our hand in our writing. Our life written down in front of us, recorded for ourselves and future readers.

My daughter wants to start a card company to compete with Hallmark. She plans big for her Homaid Equals a Smile card company. Her pattern remains similar, one day she will find a formula to market her cards. A book is in her lap - often. Good readers make good writers; they have in essence studied others writing for some time.

They begin modeling their structure and pace, adding their unique voice to the page. A greeting card features this aspect of a writer. She colors in setting using words appropriate to the recipient. She practices for the day her card company is up and running.

We put our whole selves into the task at hand. Writing takes time and energy. Our time, energy and talent are reflected in our words, our greeting cards, and books. Writing opens up worlds for each of us.

Two cards sit on my desk. One is my daughter's face done in a jigsaw pattern. In other words the pieces are scrambled. Her hair frames the picture; otherwise there is a blue eye and another blue eye down below.

She smiles amid the self portrait. Two eyebrows are also scattered among the picture. This jigsaw self portrait can be applied to coffee mugs, calendars, and even aprons - maybe hot pads to go with those aprons.

My other daughter made a flower; a bright red bulb sits inside the middle of green leaves. Both are fundraisers for the elementary school. Later I will help third graders with their reading, and then it is home for the final push on a book I've been working on for awhile. I hope to revise a few more sentences and then by tonight send it off to the publisher. Who knows how it will be received?

Having readers for our stories is exciting to ponder. Still at the end of the day, we write for ourselves, an audience of one. Ideally others enjoy our words, yet the reward is writing itself. No one else writes our story. No one has our voice, a voice trained by our own life experience, people met, places lived, stories read. Life, unique to each of us, true for all of us. We fill in the blank pages of our books in any way we choose.

Sometimes we ask for help and they have the word readily available. Last night it was the word change. The sentence needed a better word, my wife had it succinctly phrased in a matter of minutes. Seasons change, it was that simple. Editing looks for the right word and flow, the placing of words in an orderly and logical sequence.

Early on we place words to the page, which includes those distant airplanes, the shadow of our writing hand, our everyday. What we plan to write about? What details will fill our day? Whether we will purchase the jigsaw photograph of one child, or the vibrant red bulb made by our other child? Today I will help

Abby's third grade classmates read, maybe it is time better spent in this economy. The jigsaw visage and ornate bulb will wait for another day.

The final presidential debate is over. Time will tell if the final scoop is over, the one from the stock market. Our retirement accounts continue to shrink with each passing month.

Those accounts set up to ensure Americans have a planned retirement down the road. It just got postponed, extended for many Americans inside the middle of their careers. The political season reflects the absurdity on Wall Street, the weird of Washington, the current state of affairs. Like the expensive store encounter awhile back, life gets bizarre at times.

If you didn't get a chance to read my earlier book, I describe visiting a high end store in Portland. The store clerk suggests life is about choices, fifteen kids or wearing the luxurious Italian fabric. The price is luxurious, thousands of dollars for a shirt, several thousands for a jacket. As a member of a larger family, the encounter proved interesting.

Something said about family size correlating with level of education. There are smart people reporting the daily news, a smarter bunch running our financial system in the world headquarters to all - New York City. Washington DC is now done with their final debate, the people will choose in less than three weeks. People will choose, yet money plays a role alongside the individual vote.

Regrettably the middle class money has all but disappeared. The rich continue in much the same, they have million dollars buffers, several have billion dollar buffers. The poor continue life as usual; they are poor, not much changes for them. Those in the middle feel the squeeze. The overall economy will feel the result; fewer consumers mean less profit for the oil, auto, and retail companies. A vicious cycle October 2008 brought to the fore, or collapsed.

Chapter 5

Writing often starts in the middle. Once the story is told we go back and introduce what we plan to say, then conclude, or briefly recount what our message is and how it might be applied. Each of us has a story, mine starts in the middle - I'm a middle child. I have a younger sister and an older sister. Much of our writing is biographical; we write what we know, where we went and generally the experiences along the way, those sibling moments, if you will.

Often there are a few bends along the route, some planned, foreseen, others unexpected and life changing. Robert Frost phrased it as two roads diverged in a wood. Still each of us move in our own unique direction, pace, if not route itself.

Sometimes, I think of jobs past. One in particular was a night desk position; the main job requirement is keeping the front door locked. I am not sure who the door is locked for, the residents or keeping the pedestrians outside. The Tenderloin, a euphemism for a difficult part of San Francisco. Not the part most people visit or hear about, it exists nonetheless.

There are stories on those streets, there are as many inside the building, the government subsidized residential hotel. Subsidized housing, the place I kept the door locked. The people I lock in, protecting them from the outside. One in particular stands out, the whole front lobby stood out when I think about it. I would watch them come in each with their own story, their future plans, their everyday routines.

It's years later and I sit thinking how I will write this story. There is a story in this building with a piano in its lobby and residents who congregate in the early morning hours.

Music for Einstein is a personal matter; he was reluctant to play in front of others. I understand. Still I play as often as I can, even though years ago the lobby piano was off limits, as I might wake up the residents. The lobby is full of varied and poignant stories, yet time goes on - I have since moved to Oregon.

Chapter 6

A lifetime is reflected within our writing. We write what we know, what we hope to learn along the way. Lots of this week would be better in the recycle bin. Unfortunately, this part of life can't be taken back. Replayed.

Thus for many Americans a new day is upon us, a new economic reality. The last political debate is over for this season. In January, I said many will be glad to see 2008 end. By October, the end is near, not just the approaching end of the calendar. It's been ugly, yet they smile from the presidential debate podium.

As for calendars, I found three without searching my room. They were indispensable while in school, even today they keep track of our dates, some more important, others frozen in time without us checking a calendar.

The political debates are over. Some promise across the board cuts or at a minimum a freeze. This morning's newspaper mentions a five point eight percent increase in social security. A program on the brink of collapse and they raise the benefits for an age group which has age in common and one other detail, perhaps the country's wealth.

After the MCI and Enron debacle, Washington promised swift change, a safety net of sorts. Many aren't feeling secure a year later, in fact many are on the brink of collapse. Whole neighborhoods are up for sale, even more are in foreclosure.

A redistribution of wealth. Even Money magazine has a full issue on the crisis. They also have a full back page advertisement from AIG, the insurance company which asks for a government bailout. Worse yet they receive the funds. Government giving companies a safety net, a line of credit compliments of tax payers.

Write what you know, where you are. This stuff writes itself; regrettably it won't right itself in the short term, perhaps not even long term. That is the problem, worry, and crisis.

Many in middle age who followed the financial rules were burned last week; it took from our years of saving.

We are advised to place as much as possible in tax deferred accounts, yet these losses are not deductible at income tax time. Fewer will contribute going forward into a system which leaves many of us empty handed, the responsible who put money away ongoing, for our retirements.

Late in my daily routine, I pick up the newspaper from the driveway, and head to my den for the morning writing. Autumn is in the air. Oregon is greener this time of year, the autumn rains quickly give the landscape a vibrant green garden hoses can only hope to achieve. It must be something about pollutants in our water, our ground water.

The sky is blanketed with a thick layer of cloud; the layer has kept it relatively warm overnight. Fuel and oil have gone up so it requires we cut usage, or make better use of energy this winter.

The days of going away weeks at a time will wait for much later, after the election at a minimum, realistically much further down the line. Writing in the morning allows us to log in the daily routine, the outside changing seasons, or even picking up the daily paper.

It's been awhile since I've read it front to back. Much of the news is on the economy, the poor economy, the economy which struggles. One doesn't have to read the daily paper for that story. Money magazine has a whole issue devoted to the economic woes. Makes for interesting reading, or maybe not so much. I usually read this particular magazine the day it is in the mail, this month's remains on my desk, unread.

We all ask "What do I do now?" the magazine cover reads. They promise all your questions answered.

People aren't reading the daily paper, the monthly magazines, even fewer turn on their television. Who needs listening to political rhetoric, smiles behind rhetoric? People are afraid of what has happened in the past week, month, year. Change is good, let's hope the elected party brings an effective change. Many no longer trust the system.

The colors of autumn are at their best: yellow, red, orange and every shade in between. Walking along a local wooded trail is a time spent in nature. Yesterday with the splash of color it was all the more magical. Color lines our neighborhood, the street trees are in full bloom. It changes the setting of an otherwise familiar view, a familiar walk.

I edited for a few hours in our back yard, odd late October would be an ideal time to spend in our back patio. Usually the summer sun is too hot; yesterday it was perfect until the sun went down. Then it was a cold autumn night. We place ourselves within the words, even those which write themselves or tell our story.

This morning fog blankets everything outside. The kids get up, one places an order of toast, the other insists on cereal - Cheerios, Honey Nut Cheerios. They brought home their class pictures last week. Placed in ascending order in picture frames, it is fun to look back through the years: their hair changes, their outfits getting bigger, their faces similar, yet growing too. Growing each day into the adults they will someday become, living the lives they once planned and envisioned for themselves.

Many snap pictures of the autumn foliage. A friend called earlier in the week, suggesting we drive a particular golf course community. The trees are vibrant as she and her ninety six year old mom drive through the grove. It is a beautiful time of year. Yesterday I went for an hour and a half walk, and then spent time in the backyard. It was a surprise, a gift as the clear blue skies will end soon, replaced by the infamous rains of the Pacific Northwest.

This morning is my monthly children's liturgy of the word, church school for the four to nine year olds. Most Sunday messages center on God, God and his place in our lives. Today we note there is only one God, Caesar has some believing otherwise. Money is discussed there too. Some things don't change as money is a god for many today, Americans included.

Being Catholic involves believing in one God above, it also demands we respect and look out for our fellow man. In other words like the shape of the cross itself, our faith is upward directed, and as important horizontal, looking sideways making connections with people alongside us. Being a sibling to someone, perhaps. Not so much doubting, rather believing and having faith, both of which build community.

The other part of today's reading reminds us how this region of the world continues to be central to our existence. A place of faith, pain, war, poverty, even excess. The Middle East continues to make news today, continues to make history, a foliage of events continue to change everyday - the world's everyday.

Yesterday, I called my Iraqi friend. I called and left a message a few months ago. He was abroad visiting family in Denmark, his family is scattered throughout the world. Regrettably his immediate family is no longer. Like modern America, his family recently went through a breakup. A hurricane is the way he describes life a few miles away from his two children and former wife.

Life goes on, however changed, a death of sorts, a foliage although somewhat less colorful, brilliant. It hurts. It hurt listening to my friend of twenty five years, his energy zapped; he didn't have the energy to return my earlier call is how he phrases it.

His present circumstances are communicated; life isn't going well at this juncture. He said goodbye to a dear friend who had sponsored him to the United States years ago. His friend was elderly when he passed on, not so much for two other close friends who recently died both mid fifty years old. It jarred my friend, and leaves him feeling isolated, abandoned in the Florida sun. Now his wife and children are also less of his every day. I feel bad for him, helpless at the end of the telephone line, three thousand miles away.

Later I went to a Bible study of sorts; it's a program which invites people into the Catholic Church. The Catholic Church, a Christian church catholic, universal, and accessible to the masses. Last night's discussion was on prayer, whole chapters on the Our Father alone.

The Our Father, the Catholic Church's prayer. Who knew? There are several who share tidbits of Catholic doctrine I'm not aware of as a cradle Catholic. There are fourteen of us listening to the deacon lecture on prayer, prayer in all its forms. Pray incessantly goes the lesson.

There are four types of prayer: adoration, contrition, thanksgiving and supplication. Thus prayer has various forms and not just the petitioning many of us associate with praying. Prayer a direct line to heaven, a conversation with God, even when we aren't speaking, rather listening to whatever he may have in mind for us. He already knows our story, we on the other hand, not so much. We write nonetheless using words, echoing our voice, written on our pages.

There are lessons at every turn, so too for my friend who suffers the life change in Florida. Painful now, maybe one day he will see the silver lining, or how it redirects his life. Change is inevitable, growth on the other hand - optional. We decide how the end looks, what to write, who to call. Sometimes a friend in distress, sometimes a one on one with God, other days getting our thoughts on the page as the Oregon winter rains soak everything outside.

Chapter 7

---◆◇◆---

Earlier I mentioned having an older and younger sister, there are two older and two younger sisters. Middle children are shuffled within family. Often, and maybe early on search outside the family for support, encouragement. Each of us has a story, said the right way, it can even sound impressive.

My mother in law, a middle child herself, had an eventful life - part tragic, part enviable. She is among the first west coast women senior vice presidents of a national bank. Amazing. She was an amazing individual. Like us she encounters her own share of life's trials, yet she reached further and helped many along the route. A wonderful message for all as we travel through.

At the subsidized housing there was a woman named Wanda. Wanda starts life in Idaho and continues on to college. She is a precocious student, excelling early in life, even in middle age until surgery leaves her auricular nerve damaged. Sound in one ear is muffled, yet affects her whole existence. Thus the middle class Wanda I meet is in subsidized housing in San Francisco.

Wanda with the advanced college degree. Wanda, one of those in the lobby who doesn't quite fit in. Her story doesn't fit in with the rest of them. One day I ask. While I learn of her life, she helps move mine further along, she wrote parts of it if you will.

I dreamed of living a more balanced life, perhaps, a more rewarding life. The Tenderloin district doesn't fit San Francisco. The hills of Pacific Heights are unaffordable, so onward and upward to Oregon.

Yet it is Wanda who says "Move. Don't plan, just move. Make it happen for yourself!"

Ironically here I sit in Oregon, in Portland, overlooking the suburb of Happy Valley. Over the rim of the valley is the cemetery where my friend Wanda rests. I pass her often and invariably she comes to mind as I pass through running errands, or going downtown Portland.

I pass Wanda; she passed me years ago in the lobby of subsidized housing. We will talk more but suffice it to say our paths crossed on more than one occasion. Onward with the story which gets back to family where we start, be it middle, older, or younger children. We are molded, formed within family, even those who write on their grade school family banners Sibling To: No One.

Still it is often the people met along the way who ultimately influence or even redirect our lives. The lucky among us get a chance to help someone else along the way - mentoring.

Chapter 8

------·⟨3⟩·⟨𝔈⟩·------

I'm late in my morning writing. The kids needed to be dropped off at school, a package needed to be mailed. Fed Ex Office is too expensive so it was on to the post office across town. Our new neighborhood doesn't have its own post office, one convenient for this community, thus we drive across town to send our packages. Today a fog hovers in the distance. It is beautiful, although not the safest driving condition. We drive with our headlights and hope the other vehicles see us.

Writing in the early morning our editing minds aren't fully engaged. Today I had errands to attend before sitting pen in hand. I'd gotten up early and looked at family photographs in the hallway. One a group of seventy taken from years ago along Lake Champlain. Another group of seventy taken once again on the banks of Lake Champlain.

One is my father's side of the family, the other my mother's side, both taken from years ago, both having family members no longer with us. Then I look at a family portrait from ten years ago, finally the other immediate family picture taken just months ago. One a formal setting for my parents' fiftieth wedding anniversary, the other less formal is from this past summer's celebration of their sixtieth wedding anniversary.

We are each in a T-shirt with the number sixty printed across the front. Some are orange, green or yellow, the M&M picture my sister calls it. A casual photograph with Vermont as backdrop. Jay Peak looms in the distance, as green meadow fills in the foreground. A barn and silo are also there, three shades of red barn and silo.

We write where we are, we write of our everyday: the errands ran, the packages mailed, the routine morning kid drop off at elementary school. Writing logs in our day, the activities and the reflections of activity, the reflections of photographs taken years before.

Often we pass through the hallway without much time to glance at the photographs which line its wall. They are there, and we can always take the time to see them later. Similar to the over abundance of culture in a city, we can always get to the museum, and the recital. Time passes and we still haven't taken the time to notice, to jot down our book idea, or visit with family who may have passed on by this time. Life is not stagnant like an echo it reverberates, it moves on.

Pictures on the other hand freeze a moment in time; years ago along the shores of Lake Champlain, today as I paint with words, in the early morning. Some mornings it is a bit further along, still morning, yet we ran errands first. Driven through fog on the way to mailing a timely package, perhaps a photograph, or a book inside the middle of each of us.

It's early morning; Madeline has breakfast while playing cards with mom. Abby sleeps the morning away. She came home sick yesterday from school. Midway through lunch the telephone rang, Abby cries she isn't feeling well and could I pick her up. I volunteer on Wednesday mornings in her classroom.

Groups of six read and then discuss the story. Today mom is home so I can keep the school volunteer schedule. Abby sleeps in. Madeline and mom play cards while nibbling on breakfast. I write a few pages while it is still morning.

It's cold outside, yesterday's fog has disappeared. A magazine with a photograph of Hawaii sits on my desk. The home with a deck overlooking the ocean, a mountain range off to its side. The home has an open wall to the balcony, a dining table just inside overlooking paradise. A kitchen and family room a bit further inside. An open space, an inviting space, which welcomes us anytime, especially in the Oregon autumn rain.

We write of our current situation, the breakfast card table, the sick child, our writing. Our writing takes us places, we start in the cold Northwest autumn, and go to Hawaii, or at least we look through pictures of paradise. Maybe think how it was all those years before, visiting Hawaii amid the early spring flash floods. The times lounging in the sun, sitting poolside. Other times reading on the deck overlooking acres of manicured yard, water features, walking paths and the ocean beyond.

Still the flash flooding makes that vacation memorable. "Turn around, don't drown" warns the radio. We rent a taller SUV, still the rains come quick. There are puddles everywhere, thus the news warning tourists to be vigilant. The magazine page of Hawaii sits on my desk. It invites us in, its open floor plan, and its beauty beyond the open wall. We write, thinking how it is sitting on this deck overlooking the ocean. The spot which is Hawaii - ocean breezes, rainbows and an occasional whale or three. Hawaii, lots to distract, lots to keep our interest.

The ceiling fan is the same as the one in our family room here in Oregon. The off white walls also match ours. Otherwise there is a totally different feel for the place in Hawaii, serenity perhaps not found in the daily life of many in the rest of the country. The breakfast needs to be eaten, the sick child needs attending, and the pages need writing.

Those pages might reflect a bit of the beauty which is time spent in Hawaii. We look at the magazine page, and hope one day to once again sit in this photograph first hand, place ourselves in this environment. Writing moves us closer to this placement. Still for some that place is a mirrored lake in eastern Oregon, others a once bucolic Vermont sawmill pond.

Writing places us anywhere we want. We write in the early morning as the furnace heats up the house, while we wait for coffee, or even after taking out the recyclables. It fills in the otherwise lost time in our day, our day otherwise filled with errands, attending to a sick child or dreaming of paradise.

Our pages reflect ongoing life, as it is lived today, in the present moment. Music may play in the background, yet we tell the reader the foreground, the story, what goes on in our life. Sometimes it is about what happened long ago. The stuff we tell strangers, those life defining moments which stop us in our tracks. Physically stop us and not so much just a pause in our thoughts.

Writing happens in moments. We fill a page of our morning moments, our everyday routine, the people met, and our thoughts which change throughout the day. Those thoughts which stay with us from books read. I have several books on my desk. I've often read a book cover to cover, one book at a time. Recently, I've found myself midway through several.

Differing plots add to my own writing. One on the mechanics of the piano, even how the piano changed life a hundred years ago. Another is on how music affects us, specifically what happens in the brain while listening to or playing music. Another book inspires audiences; it's a self help book on giving presentations. Writing doesn't have the advantage of body language or props. Another is creating the work we love; in essence we live our work, or at least the lucky among us who integrate life into our work - our passion.

Goodwill is my favorite bookstore; I leave with many books which are gently used. This store allows me to leave with an armful, guilt free. I found one on writing the other day; it suggests story is a promise. In other words stories require a commitment on our part to tell a good story, to write a good story, a complete story.

Another is *Financial Planning Demystified*, a timely read, considering how the economy performed this past year. Many feel the sting of the drop in the stock market, along with the housing market.

The book on the bottom of the stack is *The Tao of Physics*. I never took physics class. Physiology won in high school, an advanced biology course which answers many questions on how our bodies function. Physics had to wait and thus I am not familiar with many of its more basic principles.

Reading only a few pages, it sounds like they are tying modern day physics to the ancient eastern Tao principles. An interesting take on the otherwise dry mathematical physics; physics the most mathematical of sciences. Those are on my desk waiting to be read further, still the daily pages get written, before, during and after the day's routine.

We make time to place our words on the page; it's our story to write. We use our words, echoing our voice and the once planned life which takes on a life of its own revealed through writing.

It's foggy this morning, the kids are dropped off at school. One has physical education, the other, music. Each day there is an extra class to add variety to their routine. The daily paper waits by the front door. Today we are all on a later schedule, the days are shorter and so the nights seem short as well.

The leaves are at their best. We will go to a local golf course community tomorrow for their Halloween festivities. The community a neighbor called about last week, the one with the tree lined winding road at its entrance, and throughout its leafy neighborhood.

Many whose funds are down thirty five percent this year might enjoy the foliage as distraction. This year will not be regarded well in history books. Closer to home I lost two aunts and an uncle this past year. A new great nephew was born last month, still the older generation leaves at a quickened pace.

Time for change, the national stage is set for change as well. A ballot sits on my desk. My wife has hers sealed and ready to be mailed. I will stamp it and drop in the mail along with mine which is nearby. Voting matters, although many feel shortchanged.

Millions of dollars spent on campaigns. Let's hope common sense returns to Washington, common sense and justice for Wall Street as well.

Many parts of the country struggle, the housing markets in: Florida, Arizona, Nevada, Ohio, and Michigan. The retirement saving accounts struggle too for the lucky among us who save diligently, meaning years of work along the way. Many rely on government to fund their everyday. Still it's regrettable America has gone amok.

A quick visit to Las Vegas, maybe Orlando is a reminder of our prosperous America - or not. Americans begin to be the minority tourist in our own country, something about foreigners being able to afford more. The United States losing its stature as a leader, its competitive edge.

Not a good day for America. The fog is outside; it seems much of the country is fogged in a malaise - an economic and political malaise.

Chapter 9

Sharing what we know is one of life's treasures. Siblings add to the daily learning curve. Along with those two younger and two older sisters, I also have a younger and an older brother. Did I say a middle child? By now you get an idea of middle, sometimes it seems lodged inside, in the middle.

Each of us has a story, some start off earlier than others. They are forced along by their circumstances and ideally find mentors along the route. I joined the service at seventeen and it was a pivotal point in my life. Following orders came easily enough; maybe being stuck in the middle has its merits.

Roger was another resident in the subsidized housing. Like my friend Wanda, he doesn't fit in either. Yet he is right there inside the middle. He once was at the front of the line, initially, at least. Early on he attends college and becomes an engineer. He worked at IBM; he was at the cutting edge of computer technology. Roger is a whiz kid. Roger is smart. Roger gets it.

He then gets a hold of drugs and drugs take a hold of him, that's Roger's story. Yet if a crisis developed, I would rely on him. He could always fix things. Although on my first night on the job at the subsidized housing I had to call the fire department. Until then, I had never dialed 911. I called the San Francisco city fire department the first night on the graveyard shift, it kept me wide awake.

This particular night I am wide awake and so is Roger trying to fix a water leak. Yet even he can't stop the water. In the meantime we talk, we both have east coast roots, start life in a similar way, go to college and hope for a better future. Roger doesn't fit in, much like a lot of the people in this residential hotel; even the Tenderloin doesn't fit within San Francisco.

Each person in the lobby has a story. Each person has a different route, a different schedule. I met with each of them individually. Wanda, Roger and those you'll meet in the coming chapters. Words color our story, even those which write themselves as they echo our past, reveal our current day, and further our story.

Chapter 10

---·◈·---

A plane flies over as I dosed off into sleep last night, a plane flies overhead this morning waking me up. I'd gone to bed early. Today is the Halloween festivities for children at a nearby golf course community.

Regrettably none of this is unusual. There are cycles to politics, the economy, and life. Still these are tough economic times. The daily paper sits outside our door and the doorstep of neighbors. Perhaps we will stop that subscription too. Who needs to read further of the United State's plight? Still to blame the top is not fair; there are three governing bodies, a balance of power.

As for the economic mess, many suggest turning off the news. While on jury duty last month I started to read a book on pianos, the selling, and refurbishing of them. How pianos came about and how they continue to influence our life.

It took a while to read through. The gist of the book, pianos like music itself take us places, they hold our moments, reflect memories of moments past, and play our music.

A piano, in good times and not so good times, still yields music, memories and moments. Music while playing the keys, memories as we think back on the lobby of people with a piano at our side, or even those moments we read of another's piano experience.

We must make the effort to sit at its keyboard and empty ourselves is how it is phrased. In essence people play, or hear music long before they strike the first note. Quieting ourselves is a good start to most any activity, even dosing off to sleep with the hum of a distant plane.

The Halloween festivity at a local golf course over, the kids wash off turtles and frogs painted down the sides of their face. The hair coloring also gets washed off. Thought we might go to the beach, yet late last night someone called and requested Madeline fill in for their child who is sick. We are up earlier than usual to fill today's church altar serving commitment, which requires the black nails must go as well.

We are up early to fit in breakfast. I write in the early morning, coffee by my side as paper and books crowd my desk. I finish reading a book, one I started a month ago. It took awhile to read through, always wonder if this matches how authors write. Do they write at a fast clip, or does it take them along then stopping, maybe weeks at a time before they continue writing? Pausing in their thoughts, depending on what is happening in their lives?

Suppose each book is different, each writer's pace unique. The important thing is the book is written, the book is read, or in the case of the last book read, the piano is played. The author took lessons in his youth and rekindled this passion as an adult; an adult who now plays for the love of music, not so much for an audience, a teacher, or his parents.

True music is first played for ourselves, only later do others hear and appreciate our unique sound. So too with writing, we write for an audience of one, ourselves. This doesn't change, whether our books end up in wide circulation, or on our own personal bookshelves.

It takes a commitment of time and a life of experience to jot something down. Often this experience is pulled from those around us. Still we write about ourselves, as it is virtually impossible to write of others without placing ourselves in the frame, a relative frame which adds credibility to writing. We write so others can read our words, hear our music, and listen in on our conversation.

Others read along sometimes recognizing the story or parts of the plot, maybe the setting is familiar. It is this part of most stories which tug at the reader, the writer places us beside him as he writes. The reader hears those overhead planes flying in the distance, the spoon tapping the rim of a breakfast bowl from the kitchen, maybe the click of our writing instrument. Other times the lobby full of conversation, sibling moments amid the Tenderloin.

The reader spends time with us, they hear what we hear, the bits of conversation coming from a kitchen a few rooms away. The cluttered desk, they see it too. They smell the coffee. Writing can pull in the reader in much the same way it initially attracts the writer. Writing engages the writer; he writes at a fast clip, other times taking a break to experience more life, more to write about later.

Writing pauses to reflect on life, ours and those around us. Those moments long since passed and yet some days a physical reminder of that time stops us in our tracks. Even thirty five years later, they affect our life, they word our books.

I spent much of yesterday outside, first a three mile walk, later in the back patio editing. Rereading a story on Las Vegas, Oscar and a neighbor's travels. Las Vegas is backdrop to the story. Yesterday the backdrop was the autumn foliage, the high sixty degrees and clear blue skies. The backyard is often too hot during the summer to spend time there mid afternoon, unfortunately we have to wait until late in the day to sit out back. Yesterday was a perfect day to spend outside, writing words.

Late autumn and some of the most beautiful weather, and brilliant sunsets before the fall rains set in. A short school week due to parent teacher conferences Thursday and Friday. Madeline has a field trip Wednesday, they will test local water, as they visit a testing site for ground water and local streams. Science out of the book, or at least for this week's field trip. Cooler this morning and they forecast mid sixty degrees again today, a beautiful fall with the leaves at their peak, many lining the path on yesterday's walk.

They add to the local mall, upgrade a few stores and introduce more restaurants. Their timing might not have been timely; surely some feel the economic pressure. People are careful with their errands, conserving fuel with fewer trips across town. We save restaurant meals for special occasions.

The mall area has two new parking garages. One is for those taking the light rail which will open next year. There have been improvements for pedestrian traffic as the enclosed mall is transformed into more of an open courtyard shopping plaza, a place to linger, eat and shop. Ideally a place accessible by public transportation, thus the extension of light rail from its main east west route. Now the light rail, Max, will connect with parts southeast of the city core.

Still we drive most anywhere. Gas has gone down to below three dollars a gallon, tempting some to perhaps take a Sunday drive. Most everything else has gone up from just a year ago, a month ago. Yesterday the scent of drying leaves was in the air, the autumn foliage reminding us of a changing season. The crisp blue sky framing nature's splash of color, the Cascade Mountains in the distance, soon their peaks will grow with accumulated snow and ice.

Each day brings a surprise if we take the time to notice. Autumn, not my favorite time of year, generally I find it colder weather and stark landscape. Yesterday was a reminder how beautiful this season is before the final change in climate. This means days of rain here in the Pacific Northwest. Wonder if the added rain has anything to do with this area's high incidence of breast cancer. Perhaps it is indeed the lack of sunshine for much of the year. Maybe we should rename the disease cantcer, add a "T" to the mix. Simplistic, still we fight the disease with no cure even today.

An airplane flies overhead. It takes a circular route today as the sound lingers, maybe clouds create the echo. Either way this plane takes a while to clear our neighborhood. Awakening to the sound of aircraft often gets our mind to drift along with those people inside the airplane, a group of people with places to go or memories of places been.

I reread notes and segments of stories I wrote a while back. One on how story writing happens, often the story begins in the middle. I wrote of being in the middle figuratively and literally within family. Middle children see the world differently, buffeted from above and below. Wedged in, they are ideal negotiators; born into this position if you will.

Other notes center on life long ago in San Francisco. A second job as a night desk clerk for subsidized housing in the Tenderloin district. A residential hotel full of rooms, rooms full of characters, each with their own story, and reason for being in subsidized housing - some more valid than others.

The character sketches are fun to reread years later. Some faces readily available, others familiar once my memory is jogged by notes. There is the handyman, once a computer geek before drugs take that life away. Another a former Reno card dealer, his morning refrain "Is it raining out?" We are in San Francisco and thus rain is seldom in the forecast. Still, he asks "Is it raining out?" One day he calls the front desk, dying a few hours later. Old age among other reasons, he is mid nineties.

Another continues on mid nineties. He is always well dressed and smokes a pipe. His stories might not have been true; his early morning schedule strictly adhered to nonetheless. He and another elderly woman, Helen, are always first to the morning lobby. The morning lobby with the donuts and vacuumed carpet. Those details keep me busy, along with making sure the front door is locked by midnight.

Through my time there I met many of the residents. Some pass through, others there for the duration. Some elderly, others not so much. They live a corner away from prosperity. Wednesday through Sunday my graveyard shift staggers my otherwise full time regular job schedule. The work is minimal yet the extra money makes life in the City by the Bay easier, having little free time makes saving easier as well.

A hotel full of people, people with a lifetime of story. The George Burns look alike from Arizona. Deborah the wild and crazy woman, literally. Stopping her at midnight is full of peril, still she sings as she steps out for the evening. Rachel opens her door scantily dressed, this is her routine. There are as many routines as residents. Stories found decades later in my desk drawer. Stories to rework, to reword, stories to finish. Stories begun long ago, which write themselves and tell a bit more of our own.

Chapter 11

————— ❧❦❧ —————

I've mentioned it before, still middle has its own meaning. Sometimes it implies deep in the middle. The best parts of a storyline are often found in the middle. So too with families, especially when a middle child speaks up. It tends to displace the otherwise orderliness of family rank and file.

I'm in the middle; my place is inside the middle. Make that two younger brothers, two younger sisters, two older brothers and two older sisters. I often think and write about family. They were always around. Finding quiet time, alone time is a challenge even today, I find this time nonetheless. I treasure time alone, would guess most middles do.

In the middle of everything was an older woman, her family ran a sawmill. Here is a woman who by all accounts has everything going for her, it left me puzzled how she lands in the Tenderloin. Where is her family? Why is she on government subsistence at this point in life, if they were successful in the Carolina logging industry?

She shakes and might have had a heart attack at one point. She shivers as she speaks. Sometimes my vacuuming isn't up to par and she lets me know. She is an older person, in her eighties, living in the Tenderloin. Had she been dropped off, abandoned? No one ever comes by or visits, at least while I work there. I talk to Helen, or more importantly she lets me know how life is going.

She is mean, is how I describe Helen, although life hasn't been kind to her. My point is I think she worked her whole life and then has it stripped away. Here she sits in the lobby being grandma. Hearing what I hear, does she think it is truth or fiction? The reality I leave after my shift, Helen is there for the duration. Maybe she witnessed something better left unseen, maybe even unspoken.

Years later I wonder if I was to visit would she still be there. Life had gone on for them; still many perhaps have since passed on. I think of Helen, Roger and Wanda. Wanda, the operation which left her a handicapped person. Roger, the drugs which reduced his life. Helen, a person crippled, I assume by a heart attack or stroke years before.

Her life is limited as she sits here surrounded by subsidized housing amid opulent San Francisco. Life just doesn't seem fair. I meet Helen early on. She likes me, but never tells me, instead she corrects my vacuuming. She wonders where the donuts are. She lets me know if things aren't up to standard, her standard. I guess we all speak up if situations don't go the way we planned. Clearly her life didn't go the way she once imagined. I feel bad for Helen, she too doesn't fit in.

Chapter 12

Often we write early in the morning, today it nears noon after a morning of errands. Earlier I went to Bank of America and Washington Mutual. The latter was recently purchased by JPMorgan Chase. They were Chase Manhattan Bank when I worked there twenty five years ago in New York City.

Today it is JPMorgan Chase. Lots of consolidation in the banking industry, consolidation in the airline industry, realistically we will see more consolidations within the automobile and other segments of our economy.

Madeline is home with a flu. Yesterday she read five hundred pages, now she lays on the family room couch reading still more.

It was the reading wolf story today for third grade children. Imagination allows the wolf to join his animal friends cow and pig to learn how to read; off to school they go in hopes of improving their reading skill. The kids learn the importance of reading, understanding we travel via the written word, travel whether reading someone else's words or writing a story of our own - a sibling at a time.

The kids take turns reading a few paragraphs. Last night we took turns reading as we studied the ending pages of the Bible. A mix of ages and geography represented in the Bible study group: the British couple who teach at Portland State University, an Atlanta transplant who converted religion recently, a Philippine couple who've been in the parish thirty years. A mix of people, each adding their own insight on the Acts of the Apostles, Luke's gospel which continues, with the hope his message resonates through the years.

Some mornings we have bagels waiting in the cupboard. We toast them and reach for the cream cheese. The oversized container in the refrigerator is expired; we spread it on and hope for the best. Then we sit at the dining room table for something different in our routine. One bagel flies off the plate, splattering cream cheese atop the carpet. Some days go like this. The kids are off school the next two days and both sleep in. I hope their day starts off better.

I am midway through a few books staring at me from atop my desk. It's exciting to start and then something comes along to take our reading time, if we allow it to happen. I've been writing and rewriting lately and this takes a lot of my time. Yesterday the publishers e-mailed they received the written material necessary to begin assembling my book.

The day before they e-mailed they had received my manuscript in the day's mail, thus the long process of having a book published is further along. Writing is a huge part; still gathering the pages in book form is part of the printing and publishing process. Then it's an even more arduous process moving it to the bookstore shelves.

This particular publisher prints on demand. They print a copy once an order is placed. Thus, it saves time, trees and money - a win for everyone. Writing takes time to get our words to the page; we sit and think about what we will write. We sometimes let an idea simmer.

We have a story yet we aren't sure how to frame it, where to begin, where to end. How to combine the different elements to the story? Who tells the story? An onlooker, maybe a group of onlookers waiting for story? Some one who has passed on, a sibling within? The night desk clerk?

Stories pull us in. We set the scene and place ourselves in this setting. Yesterday my daughter accompanied me on a few errands. Walking into a bank she remarks the place smells like mom's work. Perhaps they use the same cleaning products or air fresheners. I find the space rather confusing, taking a few moments to locate the teller windows.

Places make an impression, they leave an impression. So do people. Specifically their words linger. Sometimes it is their own story, or an overheard conversation, or even a story we word from imagination.

Remember those animals wolf, pig and cow learning to read, it would seem as plausible we humans could write about our human experience. Our very real lobby full of life stories, some playing out as planned, others off key. Like a bagel which jumps from our breakfast plate, the one with the expired cream cheese.

Today is parent teacher conferences. Both kids do well, at grade and surpass in some areas. Today is also Halloween. I hope they tell the truth on the kids' progress and not merely a trick or treat. The last day of October, the final day in a month which changed lives. Money may not make the world go round, yet for many it keeps it going nonetheless. This month has been a challenge, regardless where money is invested - it's diluted daily.

This past week we received our tax bills, both properties went up, the tax portion anyhow. Interesting one property is down over twenty thousand dollars yet the tax authority request a bigger payment this year. Change might be a good thing.

The new school across the street invites parents this morning. It's inviting to both teachers and students. Open is a word often used to describe the new space. The hundred year old cramped school building is now long gone, all that remains is the school bell. They salvage this bell, the rest of the structure in some landfill. Change rings from across the street not just from across the country in the nation's capital.

The teachers' comments center on reading and math. Writing is in there too. Skills learned in school and applied throughout life, lifelong skills as the animals wolf, cow and pig reminded us days ago as they head off to school. Learning is lifelong. Lucky students have teachers who emphasize this idea. They teach, yet they aren't the true instructors.

While they are taught through these people who lead their classroom, ultimately it is each student's responsibility to learn, to teach ourselves. Learn ongoing, throughout the daily math life brings our way, the writing and reading called forth in living each day. We read of those who lived long before, we read of current events and business proposals.

Teachers pass on those lessons. Teachers we remember long after the chalkboard is erased. Children learn in and outside the classroom, still the basics, reading, writing and arithmetic matter long term.

Applying those skills often colors how our future looks, maybe even where we settle. Who we become, this is the power of teaching. The lucky students learn alongside people who put their whole selves in the teaching, instructing of others. They understand and spend their lives passing knowledge on to others, a noble profession, and worthy cause.

Today we went in for an assessment of our kids' progress. All's well across the street at the new school. Ideally they apply what they learn later on in their lives. Learning in and outside of school, integrating the lessons learned into life.

Writing requires we place ourselves in our writing, in other words in the midst of our story, our present. Writing centers us. Last night midway through handing out candy to trick or treaters the lights went out. The kids screamed outside in the pitch dark of night. I was inside taking dictation. I spent the afternoon jogging my memory of a time long ago, decades ago as a night desk clerk. The reflection not so much on the job details, rather the people who peopled the overnight shift.

The lobby of people who congregated there every morning. People write our stories, they add to life. Early on they ask us what we plan to do. Some help define our life, they give it direction. Life is dynamic this way. It was simple enough, a night desk clerk position. Still it was much more, the setting writes itself, the

Tenderloin, a place forgotten, neglected just corners away from San Francisco's opulence. A sibling within, inside the middle.

Tourists mere blocks away shop, eat, and create new experiences. Travel gives us more to reflect on later, new sights, experiences, and people. It is people who make memories, who create relationship. So too for stories, invariably it is those we meet along the way who add to the storyline.

Learning in the classroom, learning on the job, learning within living each day, open to opportunity which may come along. Often we have to set aside time to collect our thoughts, focus our ideas, and as often, recognize the new sibling. People, words and experiences each write more of our pages.

Writing takes a while as we process our experiences. We write quickly, only later going back to see the story revealed within our written pages. It takes time. Writing allows us to reflect on the message there all along, yet in the blur of activity, we fail to see the first time through.

We log our thoughts on the page, empty ourselves of ideas, past experiences, and future hopes. We place it on the page, and later review to write down better ideas, more cogent plans, or more concise passages. More relevant stories, stories which change us whereby changing future readers. Stories valued and not simply scribbled. It takes time to learn anything of value, learning continues throughout life. Writing sees us through yet often it is rereading, and rewriting that hold promise.

Words yield the most reward. Within our words there might be something of value, something noteworthy, literally, if not figuratively, right there inside the middle.

Chapter 13

———— ✦❦✦ ————

By now you come to expect a new chapter to begin with my position within family. There are more. Younger, two brothers and two sisters. Older two brothers and four sisters. Middle, I know middle. Sibling To: No One wasn't my grade school family banner!

To continue through the middle of our story, it's not so much what happens rather what happens within. In other words, do we become lodged, stuck or adjust our footing and carry on. Sometimes it takes a larger part of life, before we recognize this. Simply put, many are held back and aren't even aware of it. Faulkner wrote on this idea.

The Moviegoer was one of the books read for book club; a book club which implodes once we each write our own story. Writing is a quick way to meet people. Many prefer to distance themselves from such honesty. Being an orphan is not an easy story to tell. That day, middle doesn't seem so difficult.

Two others wrote of being the youngest. So it goes, each of us has a story, whether or not we take the time to write it down in book form. Stories start within family, even those whose elementary school banners read Sibling To: No One.

I have no idea where he fit in, yet George, the George Burns look alike from the Tempe, Arizona area was usually up to mischief. He would leave and the rule is the door is locked; you are out for the night. Often I would break the rule and let them back in, should they come back after midnight.

Still George is one of those who left around eleven pm. Here is a sixty year old, I assume an alcoholic. I don't know why he lives in subsidized housing. He left Arizona years earlier and ends in subsidized housing on the west coast. He reminds me of George Burns, the guy has a certain look - his oversized glasses, his demeanor. He is a funny character and I am sure there is an equally funny story; I never learn the gist of his.

Wanda I know well, our lives parallel. Roger likewise is familiar. Helen is a lot older so we wouldn't necessarily have much in common. George leaves me puzzled. I think it is safe to say alcohol is his beverage of choice, and dictates his future. I don't know where he is along in life, before alcohol takes whatever remains. So here he sits inside the middle, listening to the morning lobby chatter.

They each have their positions, hopes, and routines. Each morning they get up and come down through the lobby and continue on with their day. Their day which is living in the Tenderloin amid subsidized housing. George is among the middle of them.

Chapter 14

Today we turn clocks back one hour, it gives us an extra hour to use anyway we choose. Many sleep in longer. The morning paper waits outside in the autumn rain. The leaves are at their peak, many fall along the sidewalks outside, while others cover the wooden trail I walked yesterday.

Colorful orange, red, and yellow leaves drape the wood bridge supporting part of the trail. Rather than the usual wood planks and surrounding bare rock walls which line the path, it is a colorful autumn draped landscape.

Surprises me with its color, the falling leaves a reminder of the cycles in nature, cycles in life. The daily paper has one last attempt to sway voters, reporting on our voting thus far. News not so newsworthy of late, or credible for that matter.

We wake up later, the changing of clocks changes our rhythm. We sleep in, or take the day a bit slower than usual. Last month is one for the history books. Many happy the month that was October 2008 is over. Can it get any worse? Apparently this year anything is possible.

We go forward; we write what occurs in our lives, in the lives of others. What goes on around the world and in our part of the world? We stop to notice the outside noises, yet we continue to write, to log in our ideas. Yesterday I typed more of a book I'm in the middle of writing.

Inside, in the Middle is its initial title. Parts of the story are biographical. I'm a middle child, like San Francisco's Tenderloin district, it too is in the middle, the bleak, often forgotten middle.

Perhaps the independent middle, the one with less representation, thus it stands on its own.

Middles, the mediators, those born negotiating. Above and below they are crowded in the middle, inside. Thus it is a story of a job I had years ago within this otherwise bleak few blocks amid prosperous San Francisco. Not so much about the neighborhood, rather the people met, the people who people the Tenderloin.

The people caught in the middle, inside the middle. In some ways forgotten, maybe even discarded. Thrown away by family, society, sometimes themselves by the choices made along the way. Other times life makes that choice, thus they end up inside the Tenderloin, our books, and inside our hearts.

The clocks are turned back an hour. I sit writing a few pages before the day begins in earnest. Traffic moves outside as people head off for the start of a new work week. Another plane passes in the distance. Fall is here, half the leaves are scattered on the ground, while other ones cling to the colorful trees. A rain or wind storm will drop the rest of them. Seasons change, time to change our clocks, adjusts our schedules, maybe turn a new leaf.

Saints was the topic at last night's lecture. The recurring theme is they were once human, yet lived with God like qualities. Qualities each of us have and somehow abandon, forget along the way. Like everything else it's not so much doing one great thing, writing one novel, or a hit single, rather the string of not so great songs counts too, provided we place our whole selves in the effort.

Dedicated, engaged and disciplined enough to see the project through. To live out our lives in their fullest. Committing to make it the best for ourselves and others along the way. Each saint is remembered for differing causes.

Their special day is the day they die, or more to the point, the day they are born into eternal life. Still what they do while on earth earns them sainthood. Like the rest of us, it's not so much a huge success or anything else major or outstanding; rather standing throughout life.

Going the distance, doing the little things well: thoroughly paying attention to details, paying attention to ourselves, and others. Despite the distracting airplanes overhead or those vehicles in our collective memory which carry stories of their own. The planes, the boats, the logging trucks that don't return with their cargo, sometimes including our loved ones. Thus we carry a sibling within.

Writing takes in the everyday, the lectures we attend, the books read, maybe even the music we listen to and the people met. We listen in, and write along. Writing lets us think back or pause in the everyday routine. It gives us a chance to get things right, to give our days another try, maybe learn something and implement it going forward.

A small inconsequential detail years later matures to a huge shift in our every day living, ours and those we come in contact with. Growing, learning along life's path and circulating, so others can benefit from our insight. The Tenderloin, often forgotten has its share of lessons, its share of once productive people. Life cripples some in the group, some days it seems to get the best of us.

Today is Election Day, may the best candidates get elected regardless of speeches, funds or entanglements. Much of politics is suspect even in the United States. Traveling reminds us of the imbalance in the world. While there is plenty to go around, some lack adequate food, clothing and shelter. Education might be a luxury for those on mere subsistence; still circulating knowledge and skills moves this world away from poverty.

The Tenderloin has residents who once thrived, sad to see lives reduced to government as immediate family. There is a safety net for a reason; still there are too many living in the figurative Tenderloin district, around the corner from prosperity. Pick a corner and walk beyond, takes insight, effort, and often requires financial resources. Like politics, it is much easier to deal with life if we have sufficient funds; funds for the basics and perhaps a few nonessentials, those things that add variety to life.

Our ideas flow in the early morning. Later we might be preoccupied with routine or those things needed to get done. Our recycling recently changed its method. Before we sorted plastic, paper, and even cardboard. The new bin allows one combined heap, thus perhaps more will recycle as they simplify the process.

Still many of us carry a lot of junk in the trunk. We hang on to paperwork much longer than we should, or need. The school projects, magazines, the newspapers, it accumulates a day at a time, one mailing at a time. It's good on occasion to clear house, even the political landscape should be changed from time to time.

One could argue candidates should look like their constituents, live like their constituents. No longer the case in America, perhaps it is no longer feasible as elections often require monetary resources. Regrettably some of the otherwise more qualified don't run for office.

Why bother they ask themselves? Like the Tenderloin group, after awhile one just settles in and accepts what life has thrown their way. Who knows, maybe some write about it, their present and future plans for themselves and those around them.

Still their present or even their past isn't so wonderful. Trapped inside the middle. Not the radical middle, rather stuck there with fewer options. Life can be taken from people long before they pass on.

Even in prosperous America, life can be difficult. Food, water, clothing and shelter are not always readily available worldwide, much less in America. In America on Election Day; an election that approaches spending a billion dollars or more. Be sure to vote.

A helicopter hovers above. It is back to Alaska for Governor Palin. "She's from Wasilla," said my friend in disgust. Where people are from forms them, still where they are headed matters. Learning what happens early in someone's life often defines how their life plays out. For some it is the Tenderloin, others onward and upward in spite of hometown or media support.

A garbage truck shifts outside. The kids finish breakfast a room away; I'm in the den writing a few pages in the early morning. The not so early morning as we get accustomed to the change to daylight savings time. I deliver a dozen roses to neighbors as they celebrate their forty eighth wedding anniversary. Another neighbor celebrates a late forties birthday - unemployed. My nephew shares her birthday and I hope his life is more balanced. Unemployment permeates our whole existence, our being. I wrote a book on being unemployed while searching for meaningful work and our place in the sun.

The shadow of my hand continues moving along the page. Writing is a time to quiet down and listen. The garbage truck is back, perhaps collecting recyclables this go round. It is a mixed sound of crushing bottles and truck engine, the occasional roll of a dumpster, routine to our Thursday. The Oregon rains are here this morning, like routine they will keep everything green during this otherwise cold wet season.

We write of our routine and those parts of our day that aren't; the trips to Costco for the anniversary bouquet, the stop at the barber. The mail carrier varies his schedule, late afternoon now replaces the more prompt eleven am delivery. Makes it convenient to mail outgoing correspondence, not so convenient to work on the late daily incoming mail. Our schedules, our routines adapt accordingly.

Wednesday is reading time with third grade students. I volunteer in our daughter's class once a week. Yesterday they drew pictures of a book they recently read. There is a circle cut up in six pie slices. The center circle holds the book title, author and student name. The first slice covers the main character, the second - the setting. The third, the antagonist. The fourth, the main problem in the story. They are to skip over this section. The fifth, the solution to the problem. The sixth asks why the author writes the book, and is the author effective in conveying his message. A visual of a book.

I suggest to them that they have written a book without using words. Perhaps the writer starts writing by looking at a picture of his story wheel. Insight on how authors write. They see in pictures and translate in words, translating their pictures, their stories in words so we can better appreciate what they see, hear and pass on to the rest of us. Words write their story, tell their story, even those begun in pictures.

Chapter 15

You probably think we are done with family positioning. This space is kept for us throughout life. Some suggest the easiest route is to follow in the family business, family line. I would argue getting beyond our family positioning is equal reward.

While it is rarely achieved within family, one hopes in the outside world we choose our positioning. We choose whether to lead, follow or at a minimum get out of the way.

This story starts in the middle, by now you better understand what I mean when I say middle. Make that four younger siblings, two brothers and two sisters, eight older siblings, four brothers and four sisters. Stuck in the middle, you get the idea. Actually the idea is to move on, onward and upward, often it requires moving outside beyond the middle. Embracing life and the future potential it holds for each of us. True for even those who are only children, sometimes noted on school banners as Sibling To: No One.

Moving on is just what Walter did. Walter has the red shoes; he is a mover and shaker. He claims he did Joan Rivers' hair on her wedding day. Walter has many stories, some perhaps are true. He is in subsidized housing although Walter makes things happen. I don't know why he lives here. Economically it makes sense, everyone can afford subsidized housing. Still he doesn't fit in.

Walter gives tours to the tourists who come to San Francisco; perhaps it is the Gray line. You can be assured it is one memorable tour. He has a way of telling a story, he dresses a story. There are the red shoes, Walter with the jet black hair. Walter doesn't fit in the Tenderloin, he doesn't fit in San Francisco. He stands out. Perhaps, there should be more Walters in the world.

Following the crowd is a quick way to go nowhere. Walter makes me laugh; he helps a lot of people live. I don't know why he left Long Island, whatever happened to him long before. Walter makes the best of a bad situation. Life in the Tenderloin, in subsidized housing is not the best of situations, yet Walter still has a smile on his face.

Walter makes a lot of us smile. He makes us think; think about life, our positioning, our current situation. When Walter is in the lobby, the conversation is livelier, it is more colorful. Walter stirs things up, at the same time is ironically one of the more dependable and responsible people in that front lobby.

He is probably in his sixties and in his own way making a difference in the world. Once you meet Walter, you never forget him. Even today I think of the red shoes, the jet black dyed hair, but there is more, so much more beyond the costume as I write this near Halloween.

Certainly if Walter is still alive, he celebrates. Everyday is holiday for Walter; still he treats people as best he can. A sibling of sorts within the lobby mix of people challenged by life.

Again Walter doesn't fit in. A recurrent theme, people who don't fit into their setting, yet they too write our books. Walter should not have landed there, yet he did. He makes the best of a bad situation. We all do. We make the most of our situation; while we keep the door locked to subsidized housing, while we reflect on times past, reflect on our position in life, amid the autumn Oregon splendor. Fiction is without limit.

Chapter 16

Some days go like clockwork, or better yet we turn the clock back gaining an hour, an hour to sleep in, to revise, or do whatever we want. Some days don't go as planned. We look for the bank statement, the one we balanced just days before. We look in our desk drawer, through our file cabinets, and only later amid the other papers on our desk do we recognize the back of the envelope.

The envelope we used to balance our bank account. Thus the statement is right in front of us, on our desk, on our desk upside down. All writing starts somewhere, in a distant roar of a train, a plane flying overhead, even the overturned bank statement which cost us time in searching. Other times we have a neat picture wheel of the story we want to paint, to write, the story begun in pictures.

Watching a movie the other night on celebrations, two daughters go through life without a mom. One celebrates throughout and hopes someone comes along to support her perilous habits. The other, the responsible older sister makes sure life goes smoothly for others.

Thus she is always a bridesmaid. There are several weddings and details of how they raised themselves through the years. My youngest daughter says she prefers weddings, although she does not remember how many she's attended.

My oldest daughter remarks that funerals are her celebration of choice. Then my youngest chimes in they are ok, even pleasurable provided the person who passes on was mean. Those funerals are more tolerable, more inviting. Writing recalls the everyday, the routine and the not so random remarks made throughout the day.

We watch television to learn more of the economy. The political season is over, yet a new political cycle begins. Let's hope a new economic cycle shows up soon as well. Since last October many feel the constraint, not a good time to serve America's middle. Thus the profitable, hugely profitable marts, which speak to our economic malaise.

A country of one stop shoppers, cheap and for the masses. Most products made abroad. America the once prosperous country, now in decline, a steep decline. We write where we go, who we meet along the route. Sometimes it's an e-mail from a friend, other times a comment from the television cast, or a child as they process what they hear, the people they meet, the places they go.

Early on they color their future by the books they read and the entertainment they choose. Even at a young age, we are affected by stories, our ongoing story logged in daily, whether in grade school journals or on family banners. Writing places it on the page, the good, the not so good, and ugly.

Many no doubt feel angry, shortchanged, cheated by a system set up to reward the workers, savers, the productive in the group. Instead we listen to rhetoric amid historic bailouts. Even third grade children recognize the absurdity.

The pundits continue forecasting, meanwhile we watch as the sink hole deepens. The computer generates freebies to shop or travel, a five dollar coupon here, reduced airfare there. Few care at this point and stay close to home, assuming they are able to hold on to their home. A year ago this wasn't even a consideration, today a cruel reality for many.

We write each day of our day, how it begins, ends, and what we do in the in-between time. Some days write themselves, they take on a life of their own, whether an uphill climb or a precipitous fall. Our day goes on nonetheless. We write about it, ongoing, regardless where it leads. An e-mail came in from the publishers; the front cover photograph I sent isn't the right quality.

I spent part of yesterday morning with my daughter Madeline, retaking a few pictures of nature along a winding trail. We finish before the downpour. I later call my brother in law to ask about DPI and resolution. He photographs weddings and nature, his website contains many past pictures. Ironic the front cover is the most difficult part of my story, my book.

Writing is biographical. The first attempt at writing was on my sister leaving years ago in a tragic accident when she is only five years old. The story while honest maybe shares too many details that are the challenges of growing up in Vermont, within a family of five younger and five older siblings, a middle child. There are even more, but that's for another chapter in this book.

I later wrote on Las Vegas, which leaves a story wide open. The first centers on the idea of people coming and going in our life, and the fact they never leave, living alongside each moment going forward. Meanwhile Las Vegas is a recap of all that's well in America, or maybe not so much.

Rather it is a microcosm of our strange world, a sometimes vulgar world. Bright lights, bling, amid the lack of electricity, running water, or even food. Las Vegas farkles, if you will.

My third attempt at writing a story in book form began as an e-mail. Florida, midsummer job hunting, some stories write themselves. I intend to tell my sister her daughter should write of the experience. "Why don't you do it?" my wife stops me mid e-mail. She says this often, along with, "It's called listening." That is a good last line, whether in conversation or in our own books.

I think my niece should write of her experience. Write what you know, where you are, goes the advice for writers. Still many have done a relocation or three. Same for the job, we've each had a few.

Thus why shouldn't I write the story? I write the story, or rather my niece in the summer Florida heat writes it. My sisters visiting the west coast write it. We write of our everyday, we throw it all in: our visits to central California, the central Oregon desert, and the Oregon coast. We write where we go, the people we meet along the route, those who stop in for a visit and even those who stop us in our tracks.

We write about writing itself, the process of writing, initially thinking we will send off an e-mail and stopping ourselves to write a book. Now the publishers want a better quality front cover photograph. It could be worse, they could ask for better words. Our words and stories get better with time. Writing like anything else improves with practice, whether writing a quick e-mail, a long letter, or a complete book. It logs in our thoughts, our lives. Writing records where we've been and who we've become.

We write what we know, from where we are. The where part connects with the reader. The setting pulls them in, not so much what we say, rather how we say it and from where we say it. Where we are coming from, our setting, our place in the story. Most stories have common threads, thus how we unravel our particular details keeps the reader reading along. It also keeps the writer writing.

We write where we are, the people we meet along the way, and the ones we love, those we like. We write of those we leave behind, others who leave along the way, taken by life, or more accurately death. We write what happens and as important, how we adjust going forward. We record our thoughts on the page to bring our lives in focus. We write to center ourselves, maybe center our world.

Writing often starts in the middle; we start in the middle of the story and go from there. Robert Frost thought there were only middles to stories, maybe life. Was he a middle child? We write what we know, not so much in giving advice, rather in the spirit of this is what works for me, or at a minimum what happens.

A week ago we learned about saints. We pray to God, but we ask saints to pray for us. In everyday language, we ask for their insight, guidance, and trust them as mentor as we ask them to pray for us. We ask they avail themselves to show us the path. It's nice believing someone has been before, who can enlighten the way, shoulder the burden, and maybe lighten the load. Writing lets us reflect on our life, and the lives of others.

We see if we are going in the right direction, moving along, or if we have become stagnant. Writing moves us, it moves others. It's a conversation, which helps, encourages or even mentors. Writing heals in its own way, adding insight, security and movement to our day. It takes us places and helps see where we've been, maybe even where we are headed, or need to go.

Last night the lady on crutches asked for volunteers with a youth program. Her life is devoted to helping children; her physical limitations don't limit her heart's focus. Some people step up to the plate, step out of their predicament, in spite of themselves. They make it happen. Those stories write themselves. Recently someone remarked they cry nightly. I hope they log in their story, surely it writes itself; if in fact it moves them to tears.

People enjoy a good laugh, a story of struggle moves as many. Writing where we are, what we know is the only way to write, an effective way to write as we have been there, done that. We place the reader beside us as we share details. True whether the details are painfully sad or gut wrenching funny, either way it moves people.

It moves the writer; the writer is moved by words placed on the page. We write from our unique position. Know we are never alone, others have been before, others will follow, and still we live with a sibling within.

It rains this morning. A holiday for veterans, a holiday for those who enjoy freedom. Freedom the United States hopes to continue around the world via veterans, soldiers who will someday become the veterans we honor today.

All's quiet as people take their day off from work. For many it's a leisurely pace not found in their daily work routine, a grind which starts too early. Writers write in place, there is no commute, although it takes us places. We write of where we've been, the places we hope to someday visit, the places we are in presently. Writing centers the writer, reader, and the story itself.

Each of us has a story, the details vary, yet how the story is framed differentiates writing. Where we place the reader, the setting. We've each had settings which literally set the stage for our life, thus our writing reflects that setting. We bring our pace, our writing style with us.

We bring along our heritage, thus no one else can write our story. No one can steal our story as they may jot down accurate details, yet they can't speak in our voice, they only use our verbiage, our words. No one mirrors another's writing.

We learn from others, still it is our own story to tell. Each of our own style carries through, regardless of the story written. Our words speak for us. It is our way of phrasing the story, singing the song, and making music uniquely our own. We write for ourselves, later perhaps others enjoy our cadence, pace, even storyline. Maybe parts of it resonate, as most stories allude to the interconnection of mankind. We are all in it together.

Today we honor the soldiers of past. Collectively we bring mankind further along, ideally with our words, books and actions. Sometimes it calls for defending ourselves with weapons, defending the less armed so they may benefit from democracy, a world family of civility.

Sometimes our best efforts don't turn out the way we originally intend. Wars are messy. Writing too progresses at its own pace, and often ends elsewhere. We begin writing and get distracted by the overhead planes, or the shadow of our writing pen. Maybe a national holiday breaks our routine and adds to story. Our stories get written in the rotation.

We begin and write along about something, and then we are interrupted, and carry on in another vein. Writing goes where it will, often its direction finds its way within the writing itself. Writing is, is how someone phrased it. All art is. Art happens within the doing of art. It takes us away, the artist, the writer and later the reading audience. Even on Veterans Day, a day set aside to stay home and honor those who allow us to live in freedom.

To live in freedom on Veterans Day and everyday going forward. This is the hope, although there are no guarantees. Likewise for the capitalistic economy, sometimes it runs at full steam ahead, other times not so much.

A mortgage broker from the Bellevue, Washington area called last night, we spoke at length. Her refrain is keep the faith and be patient, I wonder if she relays this message to me or reminds herself. Keep the faith and be patient say the mortgage brokers, so too for the rest of us as we celebrate Veterans Day. Many will take whichever celebration comes along.

Thanksgiving fast approaches. There is less to be thankful for a year later. Seems most everything is upside down: our homes, our retirement accounts down forty percent, in one year no less. Meanwhile our property taxes hold or even increase. The cost of living not adequately described by saying prices have gone up. Many are upside down a year later and question what is happening.

Governor Palin continues to be ridiculed. Odd a country questions the credentials of the governor of its largest state. Many don't vote and one can perhaps understand their frustrations with the system. The media, the new constituent.

Cable channels add to the variety of news venues available, still we are often better served by turning down the volume, if not the television itself. Few grasp the severity of our economy; even fewer on Wall Street have our interest at heart, or in our bank accounts.

The internet adds a new level of disconnect, the younger set connect online, a step away from reality. Virtual isolation, not an encouraging omen going forward. It elects candidates nonetheless. People prefer not hearing the truth, let's leave it for another day goes the consensus. As a country we are nearer the precipice than ever, even the Bellevue mortgage brokers realize this.

Buy low, diversify, don't put all eggs in one basket. Having lost in several baskets one wonders where the safe flight was this past year. Many wonder the same after the stock market plunges a week after national elections. Change is good; however the changes the middle class face are frightening.

We write from where we are, what we see, who we meet along the way. Sometimes it is a grandma sitting in the school atrium waiting to volunteer, helping third grade students read and make sense of what they read. A few weeks ago Marilyn sat in the nearby classroom waiting area.

We've met there three weeks now. Once discussing the reading habits of children. A lifelong skill, life changing skill learned by reading *Flat Stanley* and *The Nutcracker* in grade school. The second week we discussed the election results, those already counted, those still counting, and those who don't count anymore.

Yesterday we discussed whether I should call the gas company regarding a gas smell from the kitchen range. I wondered if that called for a visit from some appliance repair store or the gas company itself. Marilyn said to call the gas company. I did, and no leaks were detected. "Never a gas problem, unless it doesn't burn clean," the technician explained.

My wife is reassured, one less worry for us in the days of leaks, breaches, collective panic, or mania, depending on the day. Wall Street keeps close tabs as the gauge for Americans.

Depending on which television network one watches, tells a different story of the larger world reaction to things American. That General Motors, maybe Citibank, once our largest, could go under has piqued worldwide interest.

Locally the picture is dire, new subdivisions have their occasional auction. Our neighborhood has had three as it continues to grow. Six years in development, some places have for sale signs in their yard, still others vacant going through the foreclosure process.

Not a great day for Americans. Our country has been in a downward spiral for sometime. Cycles end, there is a circle to life and thus a new day must be around the bend.

Keep the faith and be patient say the Bellevue mortgage brokers. Marilyn put it in more colorful language. Frustrated, no longer works. Farkled seems a bit weak too.

Chapter 17

We have different starts in life. Our stories begin in untold, multiple ways. Then in spite of our best laid plans, they unfold in their own way, at their own pace. Solitude was hard to find back then. Even today I prefer to read in solitude.

Writing is no different; we need to set aside time to reflect. It's much more than simply filling in time, filling in pages of story, rather it is about the experiences, and people we meet along the way. Ideally we become one of those people people remember encountering along the route, even in subsidized residential hotel lobbies. A sibling within if you will.

We have an obligation to give back, whether it is in time, money or knowledge doesn't matter. Giving is the cause, the effect will nurture in its own time. Writing has the luxury of no expiration. Written words continue to mentor long after they are logged, written and read.

There was the older guy, the much older guy. He claims to have survived the San Francisco earthquake of 1906. He tells a tall tale, always dressed in a suit. Originally from the Midwest, he is the lobby's oldest resident. He keeps a rigid schedule as he smokes his pipe.

Every morning we can count on him to relate a story. I think a lot of it is the same tale. How he is the oldest? How he fought in the war? The earthquake? He is kind of a know it all. I still enjoy seeing him; it gives a sense of routine to my day.

He accompanies Helen and the other regulars in the morning lobby. The George Burns look alike, Walter on some occasions.

The lobby is always filled. Here Mr. know it all, dressed in a business suit, sits in the Tenderloin.

What transpires in his life to reduce it to subsidized housing? An older person, old enough for grown children and family, yet no one visits. I often think how sad this is as he goes on about his life. Where is his family? Where is all these people's family? Did their elementary school banners read Sibling To: No One? Here they sit in subsidized housing, how can this happen in our prosperous America, our prosperous San Francisco, in our otherwise prosperous neighborhoods.

Subsidized housing, subsidized family, subsidized lives, some had been so full early on, how can this happen? What did happen? Invariably it is a surgery, a medical emergency or complication. It is drugs, alcohol, and relationships gone bad. It is estranged family; it is a lot of disasters. Some perhaps witness scenes that scar for life. Forget scarring, these experiences leave a changed person. Getting from painful loss to an equally rewarding gain space in life is the difficult part.

Still some write about it. Some make lemonade, while others never fully recover thus sit in the lobby, a lobby I overlooked every morning, overhearing their stories. Some play the same story over and over, others add a bit more each time we meet. I enjoy Wanda's company, the bits and pieces she throws in, the colorful San Francisco she portrays. Walter also has a story telling how his tours go. The George Burns character who comes in and gives me a story of his own.

They each have a story, each as colorful as they are, as we sit in the Tenderloin amid prosperous San Francisco. Inside the middle, a story within that writes itself even a lifetime later, regardless who takes the time to write down those words.

Chapter 18

It's early morning as the kids sleep in. Today is a run to Goodwill. I will clear more from my den, the garage, and the car trunk. We sort, stash and one day act on that stash of discards, it gets recycled.

I will also get some yard work done. Writing tells of our day, maybe we pen in our future hopes and dreams. Still the everyday connects us to our writing, which connects us to our readers.

Barnes & Noble book sales are down thirty percent. A radio commentator laments his book will only sell for ten dollars this go round. He says books have become a luxury for people. Books are great, read as many as possible. Yet there are libraries full of free books, even Goodwill sells them at discounted rates.

Apparently many go this route, much to the chagrin of the radio host peddling his latest book.

My first book is at the publishers. I am not happy to hear book sales have dipped at the giant bookstore; still these rough economic times force many to cut back. Or maybe there is a glut of written material, people writing of their experience, their daily experience which in some way is foreign to them this year. "It's the economy stupid," is how it was phrased a few election cycles ago.

It's autumn with the shorter days. Mornings are colder, so too for the evenings. Leaves are scattered about, yesterday the neighbor's landscapers blew a few more in our direction. No rake for this landscape crew, instead they blow them about, on to some one else's yard, sidewalk, and property.

Writing goes there. Truth be told, I should have gone outside to remind them they just pass the debris on to others. Why not pick up the leaves and throw them away? Apparently their jerry rigged trailer is already full, full of lawn mowing equipment, blower included.

Yesterday was a trip to Goodwill. There was no line at the drop off lane. Not so for the store as people rush through looking for holiday finds, or maybe even every day essentials. There were overpriced pieces of art and rows of gently used clothing, locally Goodwill has gone uptown.

They've remodeled, and even built new mega stores. One stop shopping for clothes, books, furniture and bric and brac, the stuff we drop off at Goodwill. Still it is a sign of the times with the parking lot full.

It's been a dry fall. This past week saw record rain in places here in the often wet Pacific Northwest. Five inches at Astoria is enough to flood some of the local rivers, which in turn flood nearby roads.

Mother Nature doing what she does this time of year, what she does year round. After running an errand at the bank I stop into an estate sale. Again no easy parking as people look for bargains this time of year, especially this year.

The owners must have owned a store, lots of bric and brac, along with pieces of furniture. The stuff from those stores selling nonessentials: the cute kitchen sign, the accompanying bathroom wood sign, and the front door welcome sign.

There are quilts, mirrors and wreaths for most occasions. A few sewing machines. A larger home, full with a store's inventory. Stuff, people walking through rooms of stuff. Some make purchases, others wonder who lives here. Why the excess accumulation? They brought home the entire store!

Sometimes it's better to browse, leave a little behind. To see the foliage, hear ourselves, see ourselves within our writing. Writing of our daily routine, and those days we do things for the very first time. When was the last time you did that?

Late autumn and the leaves are apt to be off the trees, while others linger. I went for a long walk yesterday, a jogger waved from across the street. They realize I didn't recognize them from the sun's glare; nonetheless we both take advantage of the late autumn sun. Visibility in the miles, we see Mount Hood in the distance and the closer in mountain range. Later a fog covers some of the distant horizon, a beautiful day for a walk or jog.

Writers write as we walk, we think of how stories will develop, or maybe even a new storyline. Sometimes we tie old stories together. At a minimum walking is a perfect time to be alone, alone with our thoughts, nature at every turn to distract us, to pull us away.

Writers walk, more often we write as we walk along, not so much logging in events or even places visited, rather the story, the background music. Often this is where ideas start to form, or connect.

We each take our own particular hum with us no matter where we go. Whether on a walk alone or cashing in a restaurant gift certificate with family. Yesterday we used one at Applebee's. A younger sister visited earlier in July and sent a gift certificate in appreciation for showing her parts of our area, the Pacific Northwest.

My daughter Abby came home Friday with her own coupon for Applebee's. She won a lottery, a raffle at school. She says it matter of fact, like she wins those sorts of things regularly. She does. Some are luckier than others, or so it seems. Writers write about it, this is our lottery win. Many writers lose track of time within their writing. Rather than clocked work, we put ourselves in our work regardless of the time, in spite of the time constraints. It is more of a hobby, a pastime for us.

Lucky people find their particular gift and use it daily, use it daily in their work, their vocation. It comes easily to them, like winning for my third grade daughter. We get what we expect, and believe, still it requires we ask and be aware enough to recognize when we receive. Some win without ever realizing the win - the gain.

Sometimes another person points out our fortune, our fortuitous turn of events. Those losses which ironically are gains if only we see them this way. Sometimes we are the ones pointing out our fortune without us realizing it. Other times people write using our own words to tell our story.

Walking yesterday there were many outside enjoying the end of the season sunshine. Thanksgiving is near. My wife drove across town for a half priced Butterball. Even turkey dinners are reduced this year. The holiday shopping will perhaps be the least costly in years, which might not be a bad thing, less for the estate sales, or heap for Goodwill.

Fog lines the distant sky, another cold fall morning. Leaves are scattered about, some yards are raked and swept, others not so much. Editing, we go back over what we wrote to clarify or condense what we try to say, after the final edit we hope something is said.

We write for ourselves and others in the process. We write of ourselves and often include others, those we meet on our walk, those jogging from across the street, or sitting in the early morning lobby. Writers notice what happens around them. Other times we don't recognize those from across the busy street, the sun blinding our view as they wave in the distance. Some waves are more blinding than others, some more memorable than others.

We continue to write, including our experiences, or overheard bits of conversation. Today the radio shares a report of a local community doing a Green Up. Thirty seven pounds of cigarette butts later, the streets of their downtown are clean. Let's hope they keep the process going, otherwise it will soon find itself in the same condition. In the meantime they add accessible garbage cans along their downtown core.

Last night many got a tour of our church, a behind the scenes tour. Where they store the books, the garments, the bread and wine? How churches are similar, how ours is unique? We are told about the physical structure, yet it is people who make a church, and keep a church alive. There are names for the vestments, names for the containers, names for the various rooms unique to churches. Presider's chairs aren't found in many structures. Alb, chalice, sanctuary, sacristy, these are church terms. The pastor spoke on how the church changed through the years.

Once mass was celebrated in a different language, Latin. The officials didn't look at the congregation. Today more lay people are involved in the celebration. Church is alive, and changes with time. Still parts of the church physical structure remains the same, lodged in stone as it were. My daughter and her classmates listen in as our pastor recollects the various parishes he's served, his trips to Rome, Australia and the Philippines. Regardless where we travel much of the church service is the same; still the structures differ depending on where in the world they are located.

A neighbor just sped away, late in her work routine. Some Mondays are slow to start. Today the kids are dropped off early. Madeline has an application for the PTA to deliver to the front office. Abby enjoys school, still Monday is a rough day for her, physical education not her favorite class. I've told her many times it is as important as the rest of the course work; success depends on a healthy body. Without health we are handicapped, we can't enjoy all life offers.

Getting around the neighborhood is more of a challenge. Vacations are less fun if we have trouble mobilizing; even a church tour is exercise if we don't tend to our physical fitness. No one can do physical fitness for us, not even the church guy.

Fog blankets parts of the neighborhood. Today we leave for school without the violin. Madeline excited about her new shoes forgets today is music class. So we drive back home and restart our daily schedule. Backtrack if you will, some days we have to restart our routine. We get busy doing other things, distracted. Writers log in the extra steps, the side steps which contain story seeds.

A trip to Goodwill ends with a few more books. A week later both are read, atop my desk waiting to recycle. Both motivational titles with a bit of philosophy in the mix. Attitude makes all the difference says one; the other contains ideas on leadership. Accountability is by far the main ingredient in moving us into a future that holds promise - leadership.

Abby returns from her Monday physical education class sore. Maybe they push too much or don't warm up before and in between exercises. She doesn't look forward to that class. Writing in the early morning places our thoughts down on the page, usually before our day begins in earnest. Today I drop the kids off at school before starting to write. Our mind is free to go where it will in the early morning: the schedule, the routine, the rhythm of the day has yet to start. We write of our future hopes, our present, and our past. This moves us to where we are today, the stuff we write about in hindsight, in retrospect where we connect the dots.

We connect the literary dots as we write along. Soon we have written something; something not always readily apparent as we begin. Only later in the rewrite do we see recurrent themes and ideas. Our message to write, it speaks to us and we in turn write it down. We listen in on our writing.

The quiet of fall has set in; people sleep in a bit longer, the daylight takes longer to brighten things up. Often it is mid morning before I open the blinds, by then the sun is bright and provides both heat and light. We write about the extra trip to deliver a violin, we write of our day to day, we write to find what happens next.

The blinds are open once again. I spent an hour earlier watching third grade students read of a chocolate factory and miracle pills. Pills take us to Minusville, thus they make us younger, chocolate takes us to as good a place. Marilyn joins me as we wait to enter the classroom at nine this morning. We both volunteer on Wednesdays. She asks about the kitchen appliance gas leak. I tell her the gas company guy dropped by and no leak was found.

We talk about life, a weekly check in as we've grown to learn more details of each of our own lives. Today I mention there are books all around us, political folks write books, everyday people write books, writing is on the everyday.

I mention I wrote one on finding our place in the sun. She says there are plots within families, the loss of spouses, and the death of former spouses' new spouses. The lives and job adventures of our children, and reading to grade school children contain story seeds as well. Writing is a matter of logging in the everyday. The errands we run, the people met running those errands, the overheard conversations, even those on talk radio.

Today they discuss how San Francisco is in debt and the growing problem of homelessness. How it affects their economy, tourism and even the every day life of locals? Parks are no longer safe, street corners are filled with homeless people. There is a major drug problem.

In short, one of America's most scenic cities has a bad day. Not just a public relations problem, rather livability, quality of life problem. A dilemma in one of America's highest rent neighborhoods.

Today as I drive to the bank and later stop for gas, I'm thankful for Portland. Foliage is almost over this season; still it is a naturally beautiful setting. Marilyn, an only child, was born and raised here. I tell her many of my age group deliberately chose to live here. It attracts people to stay longer, not so much for San Francisco these days.

We write what happens to us, where we go, only in the rereading do we find out where we've been. Be that reading with third grade children, the routine errand to make a bank deposit, or stopping in for gas for our automobiles. Maybe visiting with another volunteer on early Wednesday mornings or a moment with a lobby full of new found siblings within the Tenderloin, inside the middle of San Francisco.

The other night at Bible study, we continued our series on the Act of the Apostles. For someone just learning to become a Catholic, the gospel of Luke followed by the Acts of the Apostles is as good a place to start. Maybe not so much learning about Catholicism, rather getting a better handle on the Bible, the Bible and its teachings. This is advice from a priest who recently celebrated his fiftieth year of ordination. Read from those sections first he says, otherwise you will soon be overburdened with the book, the book often considered a library of its own, a library of books. Books with their own stories, especially His.

Yesterday there was a note from my former college; they just received a fifty million dollar donation. It is worth writing about, even in the mass marketing vein of e-mail. Today we reach many with the written word. Like those overhead planes, the media is a much quicker and direct way of meeting the masses, feeding the masses. This year is also historic in its media influence, its media distortion. The media informing its voters.

Meanwhile the leaves are in the curbside recycle bin waiting to be carted away. So too for the plastic, cardboard and waste paper from another week of circulation. We write where we are, sometimes it is written on recycled paper, often the back side of prior story revisions. We write, knowing the process will eventually get something written.

Editing we clarify our words, our thinking, we might even rethink it. Maybe for the first time, like the concept Jesus forgives. Forgive was a new idea in his time, even today that is a challenge for many. Still forgiveness among the other traits of God in human form.

A neighbor retrieves his recycle bin. Leaves are scattered about after yesterday's rainstorm. Thanksgiving is less than a week away. The weather has been clear skies for much of the fall, now the autumn rains set in, the winter rains set in, the early spring rains.

It rains a lot in the Pacific Northwest; it rains here more than anywhere in the United States. Thus we have green lawns for much of the year and dark winters as there is rarely snow to deflect any winter light.

Much of the news focuses on the economy or lack of economic activity, or even stability at this point. Yesterday concurrent news conferences were held. One with senate leaders debating the futility of bailing out the United States' automobile companies. Until they start making products the consumer wants the Washington federal money is on hold.

Treasury Secretary Paulson spoke at length of where this country is. How it got into this financial crisis? How he plans to get us out of this economic malaise? How he plans to enact measures so it never happens again? Prevention is good, unfortunately during this lifetime, the damage is done.

Many are left helpless after trusting in systems there for them in later years. Their retirement, their everyday spending, changed. Mr. Paulson spoke at length; at the bottom of the television screen were the opponents - the divide in our federal government. Maybe split screen says it, even before they start their promises to America. Many feel cheated by the process, the mess, the solution.

Maybe one day our country will lead.

Mr. Perot said years ago, once we're broke not much else matters. As a country we will soon be there if we don't change our policies, our goals, our everyday way of doing business. America is in a downward spiral, not the ideal way to lead the free world. The media misses this message amid its commentary.

Madeline had a surprise birthday party for a classmate. Her friend was genuinely surprised and grateful. They now sleep in, in the family room. Abby joined them for the night. Later this morning they will get Krispy Kreme donuts. I may go along, a reminder of years ago seeing one of their first donut shops in Raleigh, North Carolina. My wife had a business trip to Norfolk, Virginia. After seeing the naval base city with its blocks of mermaid statues, we spent time with a college friend in Raleigh. We had flown through the North Carolina capital.

Today we will clean out the family room and prepare for next week's celebration. There is much to be thankful for, still the economy colors the mood. It drove the election, it is on people's minds, and it's still on people's minds.

Money makes the world go round, especially in capitalistic America. Madeline learned about the various government structures last week. We debated the differences in capitalism and socialism. I took the communist view and explained how that experiment had been tried.

Later talking with my wife she points out there is a third variety, socialism. I'd lumped that government in with communism. No wonder the teacher had good remarks on being socialist. Otherwise I wondered where she was coming from. What she was teaching sixth grade school children?

They also discussed the automobile industry. How they had flown in private jets asking for money? They focused on the point Detroit no longer makes a viable product. Americans aren't even buying their vehicles. Still as a tenth of our economy, we can't afford to close down this industry.

It is a heated debate. I end by reminding the kids they choose how the end looks, reading and studying influences how their lives turn out. We have a friend in subsidized living, another has a jet. Up to each of us to decide how our lives are lived.

Work hard enough and anything is possible is the crux of capitalism. Still we fly in jets alone, while others hug a lobby full of siblings within the otherwise bleak Tenderloin. Some busy writing of their experience as we watch from a desk away.

Today more people question if anything in America works, moves off the factory floor. Most products are built overseas in much cheaper labor pools. America remains a chief consumer, as a nation we have consumption down. Regrettably we no longer buy our own products, whether automobiles, clothing, maybe all too soon literature or even donuts. Krispy Kreme's lowered coffee prices in this economic crisis should go well with the donuts.

An occasional treat like those donuts years ago on the graveyard shift.

Another beautiful autumn day, perfect for taking a walk through the woods or to the bookstore. I walk the three miles to the local Barnes & Noble, it's Oregon's flagship store for this bookseller. I want to place my book on their shelves. I ask if there is a Pacific Northwest author's section. They say books are sorted by content, subject matter only. Later I meet Page.

She manages the mall store and is a wealth of information. An artist, she recognizes the selling part of our craft. Artists much prefer the doing of the art, they are artists first. While some manage to be marketing types too, most prefer to remain behind the scenes as far as pushing their wares, their words.

I continue telling Page a bit about my book and how it came about. She listens and encourages me to consider all avenues to get the book out there, writers groups, churches, locally owned bookstores. As for Barnes & Noble, no local buying allowed.

So unlike my niece and I who'd left New York years ago, it is back to the New York offices of Barnes & Noble, they are the decision makers. They need a copy of the complete book, no manuscript allowed. Also include a note as to why our book is unique or special.

Simply put, my book listens. A listening book should get their attention and ideally the reading publics. I wrote a book, part of the narrative is my life, looking for work and our place in the sun. Part of the book is a travelogue on vacations to Sacramento, Bend and the Oregon coast.

Still the part I hope resonates with readers is listening makes the difference: it writes our books, allows us to find meaningful work, and it attracts us to our own place in the sun. "It's called listening," says my wife. Life flows once we listen. Books take on a life of their own once "It's called listening" ends our story. Or begins our story, even those started in the middle, inside the middle.

Another niece also left New York and moved to San Francisco. She follows my route although one city behind. People follow us, some closer than others. They listen in as they sit beside us.

I hope Page at the bookstore takes this away as we leave each other returning to our daily routine. I thank her for taking the time to meet with me, taking the time to give advice and encouragement. Still it is not so much what we say, or even how we phrase it, rather it's what readers tell themselves as they read our words.

Writers were also lining the courtyard beside the bookstore yesterday. Fifteen of them were there for a book signing, again a wealth of information and experience. All genres of writing are represented; I spoke to several of the authors. I listened in as it were. Several begin a new venture as authors themselves.

Others had been in the writing business for awhile. One suggests he will not quit his day job, perhaps ever. Some of us think we are a book away from economic success. It is true for a few authors, a lucky small percentage whose books go on to become bestsellers. Still it is the author who must market their book. The story alone can't sell a book, initially at least. That's what I hear.

Moving our book to the publisher and through the publishing process takes time. Moving a book to bookstores and ultimately off the bookstore shelves takes even longer. Writing can happen in a moment or take a lifetime.

A realtor said much the same years ago as she marketed our home. "Either it will sell immediately or take awhile," she assures us. She spent her career in the real estate business and learns to be noncommittal in her responses.

Writing demands we take a stand. It demands we sit down and write out our thoughts and ideas, we think through our thoughts and ideas. By committing to our writing we are more apt to invite future readers to spend time with us.

We take the time, make the time to write and they in turn set aside time to read our words. Our words with the hope it resonates with them. Our words, their story sort of thing. No one can tell a story in quite the same way; neither can two people read a story in quite the same way.

We read other's words and incorporate them within our vocabulary, our life experience. Barnes & Noble require we tell them what makes our book unique or special. In reality, if a book is unique or special it would stay on the shelf as unique or special. Who wants to read unique or special? We are all different and hope to enjoy differing genres, differing points of view, even political ones, yet we look forward to relating to the familiar.

Still they require we market our books so later they might have an easier time selling them. Like the realtor from years ago, they don't want to commit early on. Books line their shelves, today unsold homes line neighborhoods. Eventually every house has a price.

Would not want to write a book with a price point. Would prefer having a book purchased regardless of pricing, in spite of price, perhaps because of story alone? Sometimes a story overheard from a residential hotel lobby in the Tenderloin, other times from the sibling within each of us.

My daughter learns of the various forms of government. As capitalists, we hope to sell at the highest price. Today as our once largest bank Citibank gets a bailout, we come to realize the rules change, rules adapt with the passage of time and events.

Chapter 19

———— ❦ ————

I am writing a story, it's my hope the middle captures your attention, interest and imagination. Writing within our own unvarnished storyline, I hope to inspire each of us to move on. To go for it, to meet the next challenge. Embrace tomorrow, if not just today, in the meantime be a sibling to someone.

Still our yesterdays influence us in more ways than we might realize. Sometimes it's not until middle age we realize how the early tragic and accidental death of a younger sibling impacts our life. We aren't done with this story.

There were actually fourteen of us. Three younger sisters, two younger brothers and those eight older siblings. Not so much what happens, rather how we adjust to what happens? Knowing where one begins often sheds light on where one comes from, literally and figuratively.

Some of us have a dozen siblings; imagine unraveling that family banner amid grade school. Thus the grade school child Grace's banner Sibling To: No One captured my imagination. Maybe that is the essence of being stopped in our tracks. It's a good thing, yet often takes someone else to point it out, akin to sharing a book if you will. It too is a risk. Risk on purpose, nonetheless.

Another talked of Wagner. His beverage of choice is alcohol, it distances him of family. He talks about his time back east; he is in his early seventies perhaps. Sometimes he brings me one of his beers and puts it in the top drawer of my desk. I am afraid I'll get caught, I will lose my job.

A job keeping the front door locked, protecting us in the Tenderloin district of San Francisco. They all have stories. Safe to say most of the people met here have their lives turned upside down, some by their own doing. Clearly Ron is as guilty as the next in this, yet he talks of Wagner.

Richard Wagner is his favorite; he attends many concerts while in Europe. I assume during the war, I am not sure how he otherwise would live in Europe. He comes in, invariably drunk, a happy drunk. There is such a thing I suppose, still his life plays out disastrously. Most of the time he is in a good mood, thinking life is good, life flows.

He is in subsidized housing yet I think he samples a lot of what San Francisco offers. There is a lot available for free, just partake in it, the tourism, the bonne vivance of the city. It is a fun town, if not as verdant and calm as suburban Happy Valley.

This is inside the middle of the city. Lots of action, all the time, especially after midnight, thus I keep the door locked. Some excitement stays out on the streets, the dangerous streets. It is amazing he finds the hotel, much less makes it home safely. A dangerous neighborhood during the day, even more so at night.

I ran to get to my job, a job keeping the front door locked. I would vacuum and make sure to collect the donuts when they came in. I also tag each door so in the morning I can go around making certain people take in their tags. If they don't I knock, knock loudly to make sure they are still with us the next morning.

It is this kind of building. Some make it, some don't but that is in another chapter, in the meantime it is all about Wagner, all about the music. Ron still dances, I think of him in a fun, comedic way.

Chapter 20

Most didn't foresee this sea change coming over America. The president elect promises change. With each familiar face joining his team, one wonders what change means. What is meant by "change?" This evasiveness happens on Pennsylvania Avenue on occasion, not just with local realtors.

Yet the bookstores demand specifics. What makes our book unique or special? Words fill the page, yet in the final analysis it is the author who pens those words, whether unique and special or even whether we are aware of the story being written. Only later we realize sometimes it is others who write our story.

Writing, filling the page with words, is the least of it. Later there is the publishing process and the store marketing, finding a sales lead for our product. Writers would often prefer to stay behind the scenes, behind the lines, even if their lines of narrative are unique or special. Tall orders as the bookshelves are lined with competition, America's capitalistic quantity.

Still we continue to write knowing our book will get written, our stories will be told. We write in the early morning autumn fog, as we drop off our kids at school. We write throughout our day. We write of our day. Later we reread our notes; notes which one day fill the pages of our books. We read of what we once thought, places we once visited. Shuttling people to the airport gets tossed in, writing incorporates it all. So too for the Vermont mill pond, the San Francisco hotel lobby, even our future hopes and dreams.

Writing takes us out of our routine. We write knowing the process of writing says something. Whether something is directly from us or merely through us is for the writing to decide, for the future readers to decipher. We set aside time to write, we set aside time to edit. Often it is later in the day, a short break which allows us to collect our thoughts and rethink thoughts we penned to the page.

Thus writing involves rewriting. Editing gets our words in order, words which flow into sentences. Words tell the story, whether or not they write themselves or we have to use our own. Stories build one paragraph at a time, later chapters form our books. We write knowing within our words there is a story, a plot finds itself within our writing exercise.

This morning there is a heavy fog, the last day before the Thanksgiving holiday. There are class pictures planned, a field trip downtown for third grade children. Abby says they will bake a cake upon returning from the class trip. Lots of activity for their last day of school before the break. Excitement is in the air, so is the heavy fog.

I wrote of a recent vacation in the Nevada desert, a week in Las Vegas. The summer heat is oppressive and in itself writes a story. I add in meeting someone outside a local dental clinic, a chance meeting with someone whose story writes it. Within the mix are our neighbors being shuttled off to the airport, their mom mentions I should write a book?

Each of us has a book inside. Each of us has one, I noted years ago, as I began a speech for speech class. Few of us set aside time to put our words down on paper, much less taking the time to format a book. We must make the time to write our story. There are stories all around should we just pause long enough to recognize them, to hear them as it were. Even those stories where we give the speech, a speech written down.

Books get written when people set aside time with their thoughts. Alone with themselves, pen in hand. We write from where we are. Setting pulls us in and keeps us writing, even in the early morning autumn fog, or the parched Nevada desert mid summer. We write until our book is complete, the story told.

Not necessarily our own story, rather the story of humanity. Life lived day to day and those lives which cripple along the way or are abruptly cut short. Two days after a fifth birthday is a life cut short, then again, long enough to write a book perhaps.

Sometimes a grade school child's banner catches our attention, while having adult discussion in an elementary school library. Last week the discussion was on Mary. They asked for facts on Mary. She is the first saint, the mother of God. She is rich, wealthy beyond purely monetary measure. Mary is full of grace.

Tonight grace is the topic of discussion. Grace is when God leans into us. He leans into us, through us, on to others. Thus grace is from God. Grace flows through us. Grace is something we give to others. I sit there staring at the banner of a student named Grace in the grade school library. She lists her parents, her home address, her interests, her hobbies, and dreams. Midway down the banner hanging from the ceiling a line reads, Sibling To: No One.

I smile as I want to blurt out what grace means to me. It is a great title to a book. It furthers my book I'm currently in the process of writing. Somehow phrased this way, being an only child isn't as coveted a position. Jesus could also say Sibling To: No One. So too for the Tenderloin, those inside the Tenderloin hotel lobby. Perhaps each of us as we shortchange ourselves.

I smile as I realize my book is further along due to Grace the elementary school child's banner, Sibling To: No One. Jesus could say the same as his life began, few would suggest he left this world Sibling To: No One.

For the readers to decide if it is the banner waving from across the room, or God leaning over to further this story. Either way, it is Grace, Wanda, Roger and Helen - even Walter. Maybe a lobby of Tenderloin residents writing alongside us inside the middle. Beside each of us, a sibling within.

It's now early morning, the early morning calm. Kids are off school. Many are out of town for the Thanksgiving holiday. Madeline's friend had her twelfth birthday party here Friday night. Today her friend is off to grandmas in Phoenix, then a few days at Disneyland.

Walt Disney among the true pioneers, his imagination leads to the world's first theme park. He sits in a park with his children and wonders why there isn't one available to keep everyone, adults included, entertained. They wait at his gates ever since.

Determination and persistence are required along the route, true for all who achieve. Then they often give back, circulate their good fortune. Dolly Parton gives high school graduates in her hometown Sevierville, Tennessee scholarships so they can continue their education.

The world rewards those who reward others. Some think the rich and famous stock pile their good fortune, yet many of the wealthy lead quiet lives and further humanity.

Quietly they pen their words. Quietly they donate their time, talent or treasure. They live their lives for others, perhaps this is how or even why they amass a fortune in the first place. They prove along the way they will continue the pipeline, the redistribution which helps mankind. They serve.

Initially they see a need goes unfilled. They study and bring about something the marketplace lacks. There are still infinite holes to fill, we just have to stop and notice. Writers write of their everyday. Singers sing of their daily experience, often their pain or joy along the route, making it personal keeps it accessible to others.

Reading a book yesterday, it said to keep the faith. Know what we know, and do it in spite of what others tell us. It works for all of us, yet it is the strong individual who follows his own directive, writes his own words, regardless what script might have been planned long before.

They go forward with their idea, it's almost as though they don't listen to others, the naysayers. They do it in spite of them.

Michael Dell is an example of going forward, to committing to his passion. Following our passion reveals our future. Too often people stay in the comfort range of other people's expectations. Thinking outside those expectations and going full steam ahead takes courage.

Sometimes we aren't even aware of the stumbling blocks. Had we known in advance the pitfalls, perhaps we would lose our enthusiasm early on. It happens, yet those aren't the success stories we read about.

Learning from others and augmenting our lives because of their lessons learned, is all reading can hope to accomplish. Good stories make us better people, a more complete community of people. Siblings within if you will. Not so much doubting, rather having faith and building community because of faith, belief. Words change people, a world of people, and one person at a time, both writers and readers of those words.

A car passes along the loop. The recycle crew has already gone through. Thanksgiving and many are inside eating, or sleeping in. I was up late last night editing a story on Las Vegas. It is part travelogue of our trip to the southern Nevada desert early July. Later in the month I gave my sisters a two day tour of the Portland area.

One community farkles, the other not so much. Also within that book we meet someone who survives World War II. We met outside a dental clinic, a happenstance meeting, one which leads to a book. It happens.

So too for the driving of our neighbors to the airport. Their mom's offhanded comment I have a computer and thus get the book written. Don't talk about it, do it sort of thing. They are off to paradise. Many have things staring at us yet in the busyness of our routine we don't see them. We are blind to opportunity.

It happens, often by the second generation. Those who land here mid life seem to treasure their freedom the most. They make the most of the opportunities found here. They run with their future, often leaving behind a cruel past, war, famine, or other injustices dealt by life. Life is never fair.

Today being Thanksgiving we have a lot to be thankful for in the United States, in spite of this year's slump, economic and otherwise. There are cycles to life and good fortune lies ahead. Many are impatient with the wait, a wait for a rescue package in current day lingo.

A neighbor just left, his car alarm going off as he starts his sport utility vehicle. This morning the engine starts, not always the case for the high school senior. Suppose more kids drive today, years ago that was for the fortunate few to drive during their high school years. It's a rite of passage not delayed for today's youth.

Today we give thanks for another year. For those of us in America it is time to stop and give thanks, to look forward to better days ahead. A time to share with family and friends, a time of sharing turkey and pumpkin pie, maybe that's why there is no outside traffic late morning on Thanksgiving.

A neighbor e-mails they haven't seen us in awhile. We have busy lives, more so this time of year. The answering machine blinks, another neighbor has a birthday party planned next weekend for both of their daughters as their birthdays are days apart. We will have cake and ice cream after an afternoon of roller skating next Saturday.

Not sure how we will celebrate my neighbor's fortieth birthday the end of this month. Add holidays and a full party schedule ahead. Many in the mood to celebrate the end of 2008. Many eager to see better times ahead, it's been that kind of year.

We write about our day, the daily phone calls, the e-mails which invite us to spend time with neighbors and friends in celebration. We celebrate birthdays. We celebrate holidays. Lately we celebrate getting through our day. A sign appears in a yard of our neighbor two houses over. No one has lived there for three years and the real estate sign is now firmly in place.

An abandoned house, never a good thing, less so for new construction. A shame the house lingers empty, there are many in our neighborhood. Our country has neighborhoods of these vacant homes, many second or third homes for people. It's been a rough year economically across the spectrum. Earlier my wife was out shopping. Earlier much earlier, the retailers pulling out all the stops to lure shoppers. The Christmas season vital to their year's profit, some stores do not survive to see this holiday shopping season.

A furniture store closed its door midyear, now the local Linen and Things is shutting its door. People aren't buying nonessentials, even restaurant meals are a treat once again. Many Americans were eating out regularly just months ago.

The holidays are among us. Turkey barely cold from Thanksgiving and the Christmas season starts to light our neighborhood. The colder weather makes it feel more like the holidays, more like year end when Portland receives its most wintry weather.

We write daily. We log in our days, our thoughts, our stories. Sometimes there are breaks for celebration, breaks for reflection, breaks to savor another day. Another day of phone invitations, e-mail invitations and the extra food treats available this time of year. The leftovers work too. Several days later and we finish off a few more rolls, a piece of turkey or three. We finish the Thanksgiving feast; friends drop by to visit while we plan the next celebration.

Today the Christmas tree is up. Decorations remind us the yearend approaches. The house no longer ghostly and orange, replaced with the greens and reds of the Christmas holiday. It gets progressively colder outside; still it is rare for Portland to have snow on the ground Christmas day. Last year was one of those rare occasions; it snowed for much of the day adding to the festive mood.

Today the laundry turns clothes clean and dry. Melissa is at Safeway getting more ingredients for her salad, a favorite and yesterday's guests ate the last of it. Our neighbors are coming over later this afternoon, thus she needs to make another salad

- pineapple, mandarin oranges, marshmallows, coconut and whipped cream. Easy to make, as easy to enjoy, maybe they are full of turkey and hope for something lighter, sweeter at a minimum.

They are off to the movies later today, a few classmates will join them and then it's home for pizza. I will drive to the beach. Depending on the weather, I may walk along the ocean. If not, there are book and outlet stores to browse, along with restaurants to take in the day at the coast.

We write of our experiences, of our guests who help with leftovers. We write of our conversations, no doubt many focus on the state of American households. Seems most are cutting back as the year progresses. Ideally we could all erase 2008 from our balance sheet; perhaps we could all use a bail out.

Not a good year, still it is the season for giving thanks. Thankful we are alive, healthy, and employed. By year end not everyone is able to say all three. We write of activity inside our home, across the street, and across the country. Writing lets us refocus our day, refocus how we will write our pages, how we plan to write our future.

Writing reflects not only our writing at hand, rather we take it all in: the expressions which catch us off guard, those which make us laugh out loud, those lines which begin our college speeches and people remember even years later. We write as we listen in; listen in to the everyday, the backdrop to writing. It gets written on the page, leftover experiences - recycled laughs, sibling moments. Inspiring a sibling within the Tenderloin, or more implausible, they influence us.

Chapter 21

We are influenced by the people we meet, some within family, others socially through school, church or work. Still others are readily available through books they've written. Books they write on themselves, others or even stories which sometimes write themselves.

Words have been around for awhile. Today the written word is challenged by competitive media. It's worth the effort to actively read, as opposed to passively view the big screen. Even the small screen, television, is larger today. More channels, arguably less content, hard to fill the twenty four hour seven day world of modern television.

Finding a practical balance is difficult, still for peace of mind it's worth the effort. No one who ventures beyond their comfort zone has time to sit for hours watching someone scream as they turn over an arbitrary numbered panel. Same for the weight loss programs which manage to make it to television, reality television.

Still we each must deal our own cards. That is what one of the residents did in Reno years before. He is in his mid nineties and wears a hat - always. "Is it raining, Is it raining outside?" he asks walking to the lobby. Every morning invariably he asks this question, "Is it raining?"

He dealt cards in Reno, his claim to fame. I visit with him, one on one. One morning the telephone rings. I go up to see him. He has trouble breathing.

My first night I call the fire department, this morning I call 911 for an ambulance. Hours later he comes down, but doesn't ask if it is raining, instead they carry him on a stretcher. They give him oxygen, among other measures, but it is his day to pass on. I remember relating this episode to a friend, my college roommate.

Inevitable. This wasn't a normal situation, it's what writes books. It is a whole house of people whose lives are turned upside down. It isn't the normal world. It is foreign to my world and perhaps my world is foreign to them. Who knows maybe they write about me?

Why would someone work a full time job, nine to five, and take an additional graveyard shift mid week for another five day shift. It is what carries me through San Francisco. It's expensive and ultimately an earthquake nudges me to move onto my original goal which is to live in the Portland area.

I tell stories, sometimes using my words, other times they write themselves. This is one of those moments when I think "Is it raining outside?" It rains a lot in Portland, not so much in San Francisco. So I don't know why he insisted on asking. He passed on, and I told my college roommate some of these people were on borrowed time.

They are out of step with society, all of them. None fit in, thus that is why we sit in subsidized housing, myself included. I keep the door locked. I hold the key. It is a job I enjoy at the time. There is a piano in the lobby. A vacuum waits nearby. Helen makes sure I run it.

To be honest some nights I don't vacuum. Does it matter? Clean carpet or not, some mornings there is even a missing donut. Who knew? Over time I know these people well. One morning they move him by stretcher as his life ends. One day he deals cards in Reno, later he lives in subsidized housing in San Francisco. How does that happen?

I don't know if he is from the San Francisco or even California area. I never ask or find out. Yet he is another person who stands out by his comment, "Is it raining out?" Still to this day I wonder what he meant. Some people never understand another person.

We hear words differently whether said in an early morning hotel lobby or written in a book which writes itself, unbeknownst to us at the time and life doesn't get any better than that.

Chapter 22

I drove to the beach yesterday. Portland was overcast as is usually the case this time of year. A cloud cover keeps the temperature in the mid fifty degree range, perfect for walking along the coast.

People with their families, themselves, and their pets, enjoy a day at the beach. Many chase the waves; I do unintentionally on four occasions. The water, the sea foam and waves all the more scenic this time of year.

Ordinarily there are small cross currents we jump across as we walk along the coast. Yesterday they were fast flowing streams, thus hugging the nearby cliffs with their rocky paths allow us to walk further along. I stop for a German pancake breakfast at the Surftides hotel restaurant before my two hour walk.

I have ordered them many times in the Portland area, perhaps the salt air makes them rise, they are always fuller and thus more appetizing at the beach. Add the ocean outside the window and maybe a Bloody Mary, it's worth the drive to the coast.

I stop into a locally owned bookstore while there; I want my recently published book on their shelves. "It's a learning adventure!" says the woman behind the counter.

She also congratulates me on writing a book. Happy she takes the time to say this, amid the business details of placing a book on their shelves and also among their late summer book signing event. She e-mails a schedule once I get home.

We will return to the beach in July, August and September, and hope to sell more books while at the coast book signing for Northwest authors. At the restaurant a couple a few tables over are absorbed in conversation. Instead of with each other, they each hold books in their lap. I stop to ask what they read, expecting both to be fiction. She reads fantasy, as he reads self improvement.

He's written through the years, mostly corporate text manuals. We discuss current day reading habits and a bit of my book. She encourages, suggesting it just might be timely considering the economy.

Reading passes our time, reading opens up time. Reading different for each of us, so too with writing. We write for ourselves first, still we hope the book buying public likes our material, the bookstores are interested enough to carry our book, our story, the one sent off to the publisher months ago.

Yesterday I drove to the beach. Today a fog covers the neighborhood. The kids were up late last night, they were up later this morning. A quick breakfast, shower and they now wait for the school bell to allow them to step further down the hall to their classrooms.

We have our routines, today the house is fuller with Thanksgiving leftovers, and presents for the next holiday. There are wrapped presents under the tree, a few scattered elsewhere waiting to be delivered to their recipients.

Still more are stacked in corners waiting to be wrapped. A bargain is hard to pass up. A few of the gifts will be from the kids, although mom was the one to notice the markdown, thus the packages stacked in our bedroom. We write of daily life, our purchases, and bargains.

We write of our day at the beach, and the days afterward. Sometimes it is neighbors dropping in for Thanksgiving leftovers and a movie, or neighbors with a fresh platter of cookies, more desserts to finish off the Thanksgiving celebration.

We turn the calendar to December this morning, the year comes to an end. I lost an aunt and an uncle in January. One a next door neighbor from my childhood years, the other the rich uncle since I can remember. He built roads with his crushed stone, a quarry business which proves timely and lucrative. Still he and my ninety six year old next door neighbor aunt Alice passed away in the same January week.

In April my neighbor two houses over passed away, another aunt, another ninety six years of life closed out in 2008. Ideally the economy will move on to brighter days. 2008, the year many asked if it could get any worse; it did for most. Those in the middle feel the greatest constraint; they keep the United States economy buoyant, although their ranks dwindle.

Like the beach days ago, there is a similar cloud cover outside. It fogs in the horizon; it covers the lit Christmas lights along the loop. A few Christmas trees are lit up along with several window ornaments. The holiday shopping season has begun already one casualty in New York - Tis the Season. Lots of problems in modern day America; America consumes. Regrettably it no longer consumes, purchases its products, its own manufacturing.

Our economy begins to feel the strain of such mass choice. We go to the lowest price salesman. The war in Iraq continues although changes are promised there too. Change, the buzz word as they introduce more familiar faces to the president elect Cabinet. A bit of Las Vegas rhetoric, it too doesn't resonate with half the country. A fog lingers over much of the heartland, in parts of the coast as well.

We write in the early morning, before the routine of life takes over. We hear the coffee pot beep, the kids pour their cereal, the pop of their toasts. We listen in to the activity a room away. Writing takes a break from routine, takes a break from life.

Writers turn the page quickly in the initial jotting down of thoughts; later in editing we turn the pages more slowly, more carefully. Making sure the words we use are appropriate, the sentences flow - the idea conveys.

Editing unifies our writing, it makes it coalesce. Later in rereading, it becomes clearer. Some days we reflect on an activity we oversaw or partook in years before, even decades before.

Gradually over time we write something important and relevant to us. We write for an audience of one. Only later are we willing to share our words, thoughts, and experiences with others once those phrases are edited to form exactly what we intend to say.

Still the story goes on, even those stories penciled in on paper, in the early morning autumn fog. The stories written long ago amid a Tenderloin hotel lobby. The stories left behind in a Vermont sawmill pond - or begun there.

Chapter 23

Moving along with this story, our lives are fuller once we commit to reading, studying. Choices make the difference within families, within lives. Many of those choices we make early on. Read, engage in a worthwhile activity.

Success isn't so much a destination, a finish line; rather it is who we become in the process. Knowing someone's story makes their success all the more rewarding and at times implausible. Then again their positioning maybe leads them to achieve, a positioning never forgotten. We each have a position we are born into. It is up to each of us how the story and ultimately life is lived. Writing is best inside the middle, so too with life, hopefully we realize this before the end approaches.

Back to the subsidized housing in San Francisco, I wonder how they land there. I wonder if some ever left. There were a few residents my age. I wonder if their stories were legitimate. Why are they on disability? Aren't they as healthy as the next person? Maybe, they challenge a system.

Unfortunately sometimes we shortchange ourselves in the process, and this was true for some. A cast of characters sit in that subsidized housing lobby. There are many, I share a few with you.

As I mentioned my immediate family is oversized and I am in the middle, which colors how we see the world going forward. I sit in Oregon years later reflecting, knowing there is a book within family, within the story of our own lives, and various jobs along the way.

People we meet. People who make our lives easier, or worse sometimes. There are lessons there too, learning from those whose lives don't play out the way we would want them and clearly the way they would want them. They influence us long after they are gone, even Wanda who rests in the cemetery just miles away from my present home.

Wanda who changed my life and yet I don't think realized her impact. Many don't then pass on. Before then, ask "Is it raining out?" We fill in pages with the lives of people met in the morning lobby. We write how their lives play out, how they played back then or even how they might look in the future. We mention our Wagners. We mention our past as computer whiz kids. We might look like George Burns.

Each of us has a story. Yet it is our story to tell with our own bent, our own viewpoint, our own slant on the story. Sometimes stories write themselves. Everyday was new storyline. These characters add variety and perhaps they wrote about me. Maybe I stood out as much.

I'm the one who held the key. The person who sat behind the desk and held the donuts. The person who pushed the vacuum cleaner. The person not allowed to play the piano for fear of waking up sleeping residents. I forget how many rooms, yet there were perhaps ten floors and sometimes all those rooms were filled.

Other times they were out for the night. While in subsidized housing, they spend money, carouse or whatever else they do late at night. I never understood their stories, their lives were foreign. Even in hindsight, I wonder how they managed, what kept them going, as bleak as it was within the lobby, that hotel lobby, that subsidized hotel lobby within San Francisco. A city I find expensive working two fulltime jobs, imagine living on disability amid all San Francisco offers.

Yet like Ron who gives me the Wagner memory, life can be a song depending on how you play it. Walter with the red shoes sings with the tourists. I can imagine what many of the tourists think after Walter gives them a tour of his city, San Francisco, most everyone's favorite.

Walter one of the stars of the city, or a booster for this region of the country. It is colorful. It paints a different picture. The landscape is different, yet the people who people its landscape are what matter.

It's perhaps what attracts us there including the Wanda's, the Roger's, all who pass through; it makes us who we are further down the road. It gives us chapters to write in our story. It gives us a wonderful backdrop to fill our story. Be it from our nuclear family, our adoptive family in subsidized housing, or life years forward when we look back and realize who we have become in spite of who we met, the positions and the places we've been.

It makes our stories more colorful, a little more real. The people we meet, the people who meet us. The people moved by our stories, those stories move people. That's the essence of this story as I look back on life years ago in subsidized housing in one of the United States' most expensive cities.

A city colorful, and just around the corner as diametrically dull, and drab. What can be more depressing than subsidized housing in the Tenderloin? A dangerous neighborhood and yet there is a kinship, a bond with people who live there, a sibling within the Tenderloin.

Their plight is familiar. Living amid the Tenderloin excitement and prosperity are a corner away. But this is the challenge for all of us, to help ourselves climb out of those situations not only for ourselves, but for those we meet along the way, even as we sit and reflect on it years later. Inside the middle, too often a sibling to no one.

Stories surround us if we'll only take the time to notice. I've considered writing a book on the residential hotel inside San Francisco's Tenderloin district for some time. Once we have a certain number of character sketches the story is written. Then we shuffle the deck of character sketches and weave them into our story.

That is the hard part. Where does the story start? Or end? Like all good stories, they start in the middle. Some days it is simple and the story writes itself. We write about what we read, or imagine. We write where we once lived which seems fiction at this point, foreign to us, foreign to our life today.

Inside the middle, is where life is lived, inside the middle. Stories start in the middle, in the midst of family, in the midst of residential hotel lobbies, in the midst of our everyday.

Sometimes it is our privilege to enhance another's life, more often it is others who add to or modify our lives. The Tenderloin district within San Francisco is aptly named, or not so much. Located in the heart of the city it is central, all bypass this region on to elsewhere.

We met a few locals within the previous chapters. I worked there and have never forgotten the experience, or the place. I remember the people met while on a graveyard shift keeping the front door locked.

Each had their story, a lobby full of life stories. Some in declining health, others make not so good personal choices along the way. Each morning many gather in the front lobby as I sit at the desk overlooking the group of residents. The donuts eaten, the vacuum back in storage, the piano quiet at my right. The front door key safely in my pocket.

Inside the middle I sit and overhear their everyday schedules, plans, future hopes, and pasts. Each has a story, yet all confined to this subsidized residential hotel amid the splendor of San Francisco. Incongruent, inside in the middle.

Years later, I think back at those times, the different jobs, the various locations, the people met in those jobs and locations, the Tenderloin included. I edit as I type more of this book.

Today I imagine I am inside the Tenderloin subsidized residential hotel lobby. I write at length about this setting. Years ago I sat a desk away in the middle of this front lobby. My job was to safeguard the front door key. Safeguard the daily early morning donut delivery, and complete the late night carpet vacuuming.

Safeguard and make life as accommodating as possible for those lodged inside in the middle.

Within our writing words begin to tell a story, a story sometimes not readily available at the start. We continue and only later share our words, thoughts, experiences with others once those words and phrases have been edited.

Most times we stop just short of finishing a story. Those penciled in early morning fog. The decades old character sketches in our desk drawer tell of how life once was, inside the middle. Even the grade school child Grace's banner catches our attention from across the grade school library. Sibling moments, a sibling within each of us.

Chapter 24

Early December and the Christmas decorations abound. Lights glisten in the early morning fog, in the early evening dusk. An e-mail last night warned others are also in a festive mood, taking advantage of people out of town for the Thanksgiving holiday. Five times they intrude our neighborhood. Each time taking jewelry, laptops, and anything else easily carried away.

I cross the street to visit with neighbors. We just spent the evening discussing Mary for our Bible study. Mary and the other saints and wise men. Regrettably most of us fail a page long test. Each correct answer noting in fact the Bible doesn't say. The Bible doesn't specifically tell whether there is a bright star. Whether Mary is rich or poor? Whether Jesus is born immediately upon arriving in Bethlehem?

There are a dozen questions, each answer readily known. Although none of them true or found in the Bible. The instructor continues noting a gift left wrapped is just that, a wrapped gift.

Up to each of us to unwrap, use the God given gifts we are entrusted with, using our lives in service to others. We are given unique gifts. One older woman just placed her father in a care facility. An only child, she is reluctant and wonders if she did the right thing.

It is time as her father needs assisted living. The decision is difficult, difficult for both, as her father is at early dementia. Still it is often more exhausting for the care giver.

I mention I am from a larger family. Often an only child seems a privileged position, yet in this circumstance it is a luxury to be inside the middle. She says there aren't other siblings to blur the decision, or uphold a move. My point is she has to shoulder it alone, not so much there will be dissention within the family, the family of siblings.

It's the holiday season. We leave with a flyer on how to celebrate the holidays in a Christian fashion. The recent shopping mall death by stampede isn't the way to go. Still in consumer America this is the season to shop, a license to spend. A rite of passage, yet few understand what is celebrated as we venture forth. America lit up, ready for the show. Even Christmas decoration business is brisk, let the lights shine, burn brightly, and glisten in the early morning fog.

The furnace kicks on in forty degree morning cold. The garbage and recyclables are curbside. The Thanksgiving turkey ready to cart away. The early December rush is on, the extended shopping hours, the gifts to mail. Christmas cards start to fill the mailbox. We write what fills our time, what fills our day. Yesterday I volunteered in Abby's third grade classroom; the group finishes reading about the chocolate factory.

The new school has lots of open space: atriums, courtyards, places to mingle, places to read with a group of third grade students. It's open and spacious, inviting teachers, students and parents alike. Many volunteers line the school corridors or work the copy rooms. Later I type more of this book on life in San Francisco, amid a residential hotel in the Tenderloin district.

The people met within, those who pass by outside. We write of today and where or even how we once spent our time. In hindsight, we might see things differently, or begin to understand them better.

Writing goes back and reviews, goes forward and plans, and lets each day unfold. We turn the page on our days, much as we write in the pages of our books. One event, one experience, one location at a time. Sometimes others write our story, even siblings who long since left us, placing themselves and eventually us readers right beside them.

The furnace now turns off; it is quiet early this morning. Papers cover my desk: an elementary school yearbook order form, a request for eight dollars cash for upcoming classroom parties, a memo on internet safety. There is a request for head room parent, although no one signed up yet to host, organize those classroom parties. There is a Blockbuster video membership card along with a local department store discount card on my desk. One expires soon, the other circulates more movies.

There is also a memo from the Red Cross partnering with State Farm Insurance and our school district. They need money as well. We are to send along emergency items placed in plastic in case of a natural disaster. They also request we send in emergency contact numbers. Lots of preparations this time of year. The calendar fills with activities. Saturday a birthday party for two neighbors, who will roller skate the day away before ice cream and cake.

Now an airplane makes its way in the distance, otherwise morning calm before the day starts anew. The kids enjoy another half hour of sleep. Even they have to wake up a week after the Thanksgiving celebrations are over. Readers Digest is back on my desk. My brother in Philadelphia subscribes us to yet another year; we are now signed up until 2015.

For years I've read Money magazine, this past week they wrote to encourage us to renew our subscription early, maybe even sign up a friend. After a twenty year subscription, I wonder if I shouldn't let it expire, its information not as timely this year.

The financial news disappoints, leaves many empty handed - the lucky who prepared for the future. A plane flies by in the distance. Somehow like this plane and the intermittent clicking of the furnace, 2008 will linger in our consciousness. It is a year which turns many of our generation's life upside down.

The media elect continues to place the debacle on the American, the average American. The one who's made poor choices along the way. To place the blame on everyday Americans stings. Home ownership has always been a stepping stone to financial success. It's hard to get ahead renting, with little or no tax plan, and no equity accumulating through the years.

Each day brings news from Washington, either they nominate someone, bail out a corporation, or maybe promise to lower taxes, especially for the middle class. They have the middle ground covered!

Regrettably there is less middle ground today. As a country divided politically, we begin to see an economic shift. Perhaps like many places across the globe we too will become a land of rich and poor, rich and poor with few in the middle. Wealth diluted this past year, hopes shortchanged, and trust in the system at ebb.

Yesterday I typed into the computer more of this book I'm in the middle of writing. It's written long hand, I edit as I type. More editing is done once the more legible computer generated sheet is printed. Page by page we go over the lines to add or delete. Sometimes whole sentences or even paragraphs stray.

The overhead plane flies by. We write amid the early morning calm, the early morning distraction flying overhead. There's a frost, white roofs line the neighborhood. Last week they asked whether Mary the mother of Jesus was rich or poor. Wealthy I say. Rich has a vulgar connotation, one of clenched fists, holding onto resources, in a pile - hoarded.

Wealthy on the other hand is two open hands, hands upright pushing outward, redirecting the goods, distributing the resources. Mary gave birth to Jesus, sharing her gift with the world, initially accepting the responsibility, later leading as the mother of Jesus. Accountability leads to leadership said a book recently. Attitude makes all the difference read another.

Later we are going to a roller skating rink with neighbors. Two celebrate birthdays this week. After a few hours we will have cake and ice cream, maybe a blister or three. It's been years since roller skating, skating for that matter. I learned to ice skate first; more memorable as it was more challenging.

Roller skating seemed easy in comparison as I already could skate, even though the surface was ice. The wood floor often provides as hard a surface, so too for the wood walls that catch our turns, our turns which didn't make it around the rink.

We buy stuffed animals for the birthday kids. Ten dollars on stuffed bears, an annual salary for much of the world. Stuffed animals symbolic of the world division. We wonder whether Mary was rich or poor. Some suggest America is poor. Specifically the United States with its wealth, monetary wealth, often comes up short spiritually.

We write of our every day observations and routines even in the early morning frost. Today a celebrity is behind bars, today, tomorrow and realistically the remainder of their life. Tragic life can go from top of the world, major endorsements and a life of leisure to prison. Choices make the difference, regardless if one later apologizes.

Chapter 25

"She has to work on fastness, slow her quickness," says my daughter. She comments on a friend's roller skating ability. This also applies to writing. Writing has movement; still there must be a handle to get the reader to read along in the first place.

Then a flow, a cadence, a story moves, says something along the way. It'd been thirty years since I put on a pair of roller skates. I learned to ice skate first. Roller skating came easier already knowing how to balance on skates, stop on skates.

The kids were able to stand hands free by the end of the two hour birthday party. Many in the group celebrate birthdays as the disc jockey plays Christmas music, interspersed with birthday greetings. The rink much larger, wider with less sharp corners is a thrill to skate. Downtown Portland looms outside its north facing glass wall. Surely the skyline lit at night would be beautiful, we skate mid afternoon, many young children among the skaters.

I enjoy the afternoon. I learned in junior high, an occasion to do something for the very first time. It took awhile to pick up speed, to feel comfortable and in control of skating. Once the memory, the muscle memory kicked in all was well and the pace quickened.

The kids sleep in as they are sore from the activity. They braced themselves the entire two hours, their hands reach for the nearby wall, or the floor to catch a tumble. Their legs tired from the new workout, their bottoms sore from many falls. It was Vermont ice for me, we learn quickly depending on the consequence.

Skating allows dangerous falls. Fall wrong just once, and we are less apt to get back up. Abby is in tears early on, she falls. She starts to move about, only later do the roller skates dictate she take things slower - then work on fastness. Writers work on momentum, our pace as we log in more story in the early morning den writing sessions. Sometimes before coffee is poured; other times after a day of roller skating.

Late this morning in getting through my regular morning writing. I had a Christmas letter to write. I jotted down notes on other details to attend. A group e-mailed they want to meet Wednesday at Starbucks. Already this week is full of extra activity - commitments.

Wednesday morning is volunteering with the third grade readers. Madeline's orchestra recital at the mall is Wednesday at noon; Abby has her regular church school Wednesday night. I hope to meet with a published author sometime Thursday.

Saturday is an afternoon party for Madeline's classmates. Saturday night dinner with neighbors. Sunday morning, the monthly children's liturgy of the word. Sunday night a bus trip to the local Grotto, The Grotto with its holiday lights and Christmas carolers. I write this in wondering if I should meet up with the group on Wednesday at Starbucks. They want to spend time later putting up church decorations, decorations outside the parking area, outside in the Northwest rain.

I write, thinking about this holiday week, packed with holiday events. Last night was dinner at a Mexican restaurant across town to see a friend off. She flies back to London and will return late February for her father's birthday. Writing logs in the daily routine, and those events and celebrations which break routine.

The Christmas letter covers a year's activity on one page. Like a resume, the extra pages sometimes blind the reader, leaving us in a blur. We get the idea; the writer's year was busy.

Still I mention: the books I wrote, the economic malaise, the political rhetoric, the career milestones. One child learns to play the violin, while the other reluctant to take another class of physical education. Still she too says it like it is.

The other day noting her friend had to work on her fastness as she learned to roller skate. Another time "You have to pick up your own sh.." she replied as I suggested it was beyond time to clean her room. Keeps it exciting, if not necessarily quiet.

We fill our early morning pages, books with our ongoing life. Sometimes we break from routine or alter our routine, which in turn gives us more to write about. Maybe we edit parts into a later story, even those we run late in writing.

The Christmas letter for 2008 is done. The initial write up fit the holiday backed page. It is outlined in Christmas stockings along the top, stars down its sides. Still the words aren't what the family can agree on, so we write another edition, and yet another revision. Abby adds hers, this goes on the back side of the narrative of our year's activities: Madeline's violin playing, Abby's reading to her stuffed animals, Melissa's hitting a career milestone - twenty years. My writing and our trips to Bend, Sacramento, Vermont, even Las Vegas is tucked within.

My writing venture scrapped from the Christmas letter; maybe readers will be able to see beyond the lines that an author wrote this year's letter. All four of us as we add bits and pieces, details of our everyday. Much of writing is persuasive, still the best writing is personal, where we place ourselves in our writing, in our letters. Perhaps it is part of the reason writing a Christmas letter is difficult. The personal part is shot after the third revision, the third recipient.

Writing personal letters to fifty or more is time consuming, and many of the year's details are the same for each letter. Thus the often generic this is what the kids are up to, how work is going, the places we travel. Sometimes we add why we visit those locations or who comes to visit us.

We visit with people via the annual Christmas letter, and take stock of our year, and lives with the hope the recipients enjoy what we relate. Maybe even hope they too pause to reflect on their year and life as they celebrate the Christmas season. Christmas a time of year which tells more of God's story, the birth of his son Jesus.

An often dark dreary time of winter when people light up their places. We invite more light into our home, and celebrate with more people, food, and festivity. Partly to offset the otherwise bleak time of year, and anticipate a new one.

We write daily as we fill out school forms, and Christmas letters. While we fill our lives with writing, we empty ourselves to be filled anew with whatever the new day brings. Today it won't be the annual Christmas letter, it is written for this year.

Madeline had her Christmas concert in the local mall yesterday; tonight there is another concert at the high school. She began playing the violin just months ago. They play a few beginner songs, intermixed with Christmas carols, as we sit in the mall beside the food court.

Many photograph their children. I bring along a small recording device. Music, a listening art, not so much something replayed via a photograph. The cameras click away, nonetheless.

A plane flies in the distance. The dryer flaps clothes dry. The list of Christmas letter recipients is on my desk along with a to do list. Today I meet an author at the Bridgeport Village Borders bookstore. We met a few weeks ago at a book signing at the mall down the street. I have since e-mailed Amalie asking if perhaps we could meet for lunch or coffee to discuss life as a writer, discuss getting books published and sold.

In the meantime, I take her advice and visit a locally owned bookstore. They will carry my book and invite me to join their summer series of book signings for Northwest authors. It's held in Lincoln City and I look forward to spending time at the beach. I bought a small recorder awhile back, one I throw in my pocket and take on walks where invariably ideas come and I haven't anything to record them.

Paper and pen work too, still it is much easier to simply record as I walk. I've found however we speak different than we write;

sometimes it's a problem translating into writing as it were. Still it preserves an idea which otherwise would be long forgotten.

We write throughout the day whether we are actually pen in hand logging words to the page. Like intermittent planes, so too for ideas we capture throughout our day. We are lucky if we jot them down as they occur.

Music plays in our memory. Some ideas linger long enough to write down and expand upon. Similar to a persistent echo heard and revealed in our writing.

We read of Flat Stanley and the Nutcracker in the early Wednesday morning third grade reading. Marilyn is there early to catch up on our Thanksgiving celebrations. She just lost a friend in the Seattle area; the doctors encourage even as late as last week. Her friend dies of cancer at age fifty nine.

It's been rough she relays. There have been several deaths of friends lately; she wonders how her third grade granddaughter handles it. We go on, even in the midst of the holiday season. We carry a sibling within, that season and each day forward. We hear their persistent echo, some days louder than others. Still other days they present us physical reminders in case we are too distracted to hear them, or listen in.

I meet with a local author across town at the Borders flagship store for Oregon. We talk about writing, not so much what we write, rather the business of writing. Open a separate bank account is Amalie's advice. It's one way to catch those loose ends, royalty checks, and the multiple sales at the local independent stores.

In an ideal world we don't have to market our books, we travel the world as we write. The publishers send a neat annual statement tracking all things financial. A Christmas letter of sorts from our publisher. Amalie is quick to point out; a writer's life doesn't work out that way, early on - maybe ever.

Still she writes for herself. She is comfortable enough not needing the financial benefits, she prefers sharing her book's message. Be open to the possibilities life throws our way, in other words step aside and let life reveal itself.

I tell her my first book is on listening. Listen to life and take it from there. I read there are only a few themes repeatedly written on. The main one is our unity, all on a journey together, a world of siblings, even a sibling within.

Like our future bestsellers, we hope and have faith someone greater than us watches from afar, guiding as we live each day. Inspiring us to use the right words, at the right time, being the right person for ourselves and those we meet. A sibling within? Amalie makes herself available. I ask about the book signings along with the publishing and marketing process.

Regardless if books sell, she enjoys meeting fellow authors at the book signings. There are bound to be a few colorful book purchasers, perhaps more to write about once the book signing is done. We talk in the upstairs corner of the Borders bookstore, the room has a computer screen with a fireplace as screen saver, and the entrance in bold letters reads INFORMATION. We sit and talk about writing, both eagerly sharing what we have learned and experienced thus far. Sharing what we know, true of writing itself.

I finish inputting more of my second edit onto the computer. I finish writing further on my experience years ago as a night desk clerk. The main job requirement is keeping the front door locked after midnight. I input my revisions, adding a sentence or three. I write one more paragraph.

I rethink the title as I write along. Sibling to the World, or maybe a World of Siblings, A Sibling Inside? I want to capture the idea of family; family within our nuclear family, family within the Tenderloin, family within all of life.

I write of the forgotten land amid San Francisco's splendor. I know the Tenderloin neighborhood well, I once worked there. Some residents start a new life, others help bring new life for people who are in perilous situations. It's not the San Francisco many envision when thinking of everyone's favorite city. It exists nonetheless, not just in San Francisco. There are figurative Tenderloins throughout our world, perhaps a corner away from our own neighborhood.

We write about it, we feature it on television programs such as Secret Millionaire. Others are inside, in the middle, living their life hoping to make a difference in someone else's life, it matters to the sibling within each of us.

I've mentioned eight of the hotel residents. I'm ninth in line in my family of birth. Ideally our story and their story is written so others can see how life plays out depending on ongoing choices and decisions. Sometimes inside the middle, being a sibling to someone works too, even on the graveyard shift inside the middle of the Tenderloin.

It too is a sibling within, inside the middle the family of forty districts which make up everyone's favorite city. San Francisco a sibling within. A typical neighborhood, half go broke and the other half don't talk to each other. Sort of like family, extended and nuclear. Or maybe the United States as this year ends.

Chapter 26

"How did you like the book?" asks Linda our Bible study leader. It hit home, twice, I think to myself. I find the narrative dark, although there are great points taken within the otherwise moving story. The last time I saw my mother in law we'd spent the remainder of the day at nearby Wallowa Lake. Linda's recommended book takes place in Oregon, the abduction at a Wallowa Lake campground.

The recent bestseller also hit home on the disappearance of a child. The author describes the days leading up to their family vacation, the drive across Oregon to the campsite and later the details of the getaway vehicle. For me the details of my sister's final days are never far from memory.

Her fifth birthday had been just two days earlier. Rather than an olive drab military vehicle with a child's red dress flapping in the wind, my narrative includes an oversized yellow polka-dotted hat with a five year old waving as she races around the road's bend with a load of logs. The late 1960's model Ford truck is there too.

The red Ford.

The white grill.

The load of wood.

The truck with a dumping contraption makes unloading heavy logs easier. There is the Vermont sawmill pond, instead of the mirrored water of eastern Oregon's Wallowa Lake. I tell Linda I find the book a difficult read, the narrative hit too close to home. The details varied, yet at the end of the day or camping trip, a child's life is lost, left behind. For me that life left behind is the start of summer vacation 1971.

But I get ahead of myself. Life has a way of interrupting or moving onward with its own timeline. I didn't tell Linda like the older child in her recommended bestseller, I too second guess the day's events. What if? Maybe had I? We go on with life - living, writing and working.

Chapter 27

Starting our own business is a dream for many. Most leave it there, in the dream phase; others take it further and run with it. They set up their web page. They print business cards. They let people know they are in business. The only thing lacking is business itself. Still the day our name pops up on Google is an exciting day. Often an equally financially rewarding day, and those days which follow.

Snow is predicted for the next few days. A cold front passes through dropping the temperatures in the teens overnight, cold by Portland standards. It's wet outside, hovering at thirty five degrees. My oldest daughter Madeline has a Christmas party later today. We plan to take the bus to The Grotto tomorrow night, more Christmas lights and carolers. Maybe the roads will be too slippery, the weather cold, cold and wet?

They sleep in as the party doesn't start until noon. Then a houseful of sixth grade classmates will visit, eat and exchange gifts. Abby will join the party. I will overlook from my den, maybe I'll close the door and turn up the music.

It's been awhile since sitting and reading, reading other's words at least. Yesterday I finished more of the second edit of life years ago in the Tenderloin. Think the title I will go with is A Sibling Within. It recounts several characters who people the Tenderloin, specifically the subsidized residential hotel within the Tenderloin. A bleak area front and center within San Francisco, inside the middle. A sibling within, if you will.

These people once thrived and then due to various reasons, settle in among the Tenderloin, the subsidized living arrangement. We write where we are and where we've been, only then are we able to see where life goes. How we change and adapt with the passage of time? Ideally we grow along the way, becoming more of who we are, who we are meant to be, unwrapping our God given gift.

Sometimes it takes longer to recognize our talents. We open our business, yet it is often midlife before we take this step. We are to trust in the process. Still setting up a website takes our business, if not life to the next level, a quantum leap personally, emotionally and financially - meaning open for business.

The morning newspaper has a cover of snow; the surrounding rooftops are also white. The front steps clean except for a triangular dusting; maybe the storm will materialize later than forecasted. The single digit cold can hold off as well.

Madeline had her classmate party yesterday, six of them spent the afternoon eating pizza, cookies and candy canes. They played, ran, and giggled. I stayed in the den editing a book on life in the Tenderloin.

While it's not an up and coming neighborhood, I wrote on how those stuck there inside the middle grew a special bond. A family of sorts, they are marooned in the middle, inside the middle of everything San Francisco offers. A corner away from prosperity, a corner away from a much different world. A privileged setting away from their bleak corner of the world.

The furnace kicks on more often this morning. We've been spared winter weather thus far. The forecasters say that is over for our region, and much of the country. Such is the weather mid December. The Christmas letter is written, it sits on my desk, along with a stack of addressed envelopes.

Later this week they will be mailed. Already the food gift pyramids are ordered from Harry and David, as well as muffins from Wolferman's. There is also the St Vincent de Paul box of groceries ready for delivery to the church.

My sister will receive a book from Amazon.com. It's one I've had on my bookshelf awhile. Julia Cameron wrote *The Artist's Way* in the 1970's. She was in artistic recovery, her words. A later book *The Right to Write*, continues to cause a stir in writing circles, the circle of elite writers, the authors among us, the authors among Julia.

She knows different, anyone can write is her point. Each of us has a story, and as important, a unique voice in which to tell our tale. Her mission in life shares the gift of writing. Julia can't give it to someone, we must take it upon ourselves. Still it helps to have someone show us the way, or open us to the possibility.

Thus I order a copy online for an older sister. She has a lifetime of experience, still she often phrases it differently. Unlike the rest of us, she writes without effort and her words flow. Then again, Julia's point is to write in our own voice, our own cadence, our own way.

I send the book to my sister so she might write, write a book or three. Use her words. As it works out, she was godmother to our sister whose voice echoes throughout this book as I write along. My sibling within, if you will.

Five inches of snow blanket the outdoors. "The wind polishes the ice," said my wife as we drove along yesterday. Today we are left with cold, artic cold with single digit temperatures overnight. The wind chill makes it feel even colder.

The snow cover brightens up an all too familiar stark, wet Pacific Northwest. The kids are off school today, realistically for the remainder of the week. The cold prevents them from being outside waiting for a bus. The mix of snow and ice prevent buses from driving the ridges of Happy Valley. Thus the new school sits idle with its snow cover and icicles.

Yesterday we made the early church service, half the congregation didn't. Surely even fewer inside the later service as the weather gets progressively worse. Madeline's middle school class trip to The Grotto is cancelled due to the nasty weather. We debate whether watching Christmas lights and listening to carolers would be worth the wait in the cold. The cancelled bus trip makes the decision for us.

We spent most of yesterday across the street eating appetizers, lunch, dinner, and cookies and appetizers. Drinks, coffee, a mix of weather outside, food, fun and conversation inside. Nearby magazines add to the discussion.

Maintenance and balance are part of life, all of life, and not simply in living a physically healthy life. We need to take ourselves on a walk. We need to embrace ourselves, carrying extra pounds around is physically not the way to go. Yet we ask the world to move aside, as though others need take our walk for us.

It was a lively debate as we ate the holiday routine of junk food. Once in awhile a healthy body resists the damage. Daily, not so much. Living a life loved is difficult depending on what happens before. We each have our own story. Some pen it to the page, others write themselves, lodged in our physical body. It too tells a story.

The snow has left the area quiet, white and deserted. Most stay inside once the sliding, sledding and snowball fights are over. It remains cold, near zero degrees wind chill overnight. Schools closed again today. Another storm with more snow expected Wednesday and Thursday. Then Friday, colder weather. Saturday and Sunday - sleet. It's a wintry week, thus school is closed. Today's work hours are shortened by two, maybe more.

We read some of my book on the Tenderloin yesterday. Madeline got a third of the way through. Abby lingered in the family room. She enjoyed parts of the story as well, especially the parts where I include their schedule and what she reads in third grade.

I mention the day she comes home early from school. She calls in sick from the school office. She cries into the phone for me to come pick her up. Yesterday she wanted Madeline to hurry along reading so they could play school; play school with their webkins.

Today the loop is closed with snow and ice. Even the mail wasn't delivered yesterday. We have thirty Christmas cards in the mailbox, they will be delayed. Delayed in leaving the Pacific Northwest, delayed in reaching New England, the bulk of them headed for Vermont.

Parts of New England have been out of electricity due to an ice storm. Parts of New Hampshire lost power for over ten days. I hope the power stays on as it's colder here too this year. Lots of damage waiting to happen should we lose electricity, the additional weight of a layer of ice damaging not only to the landscape at this point.

The kids sleep in, Melissa too. Just now the phone clicks from the kitchen. Melissa is awake calling in to see the day's work schedule. Schools are closed across the region. At eight forty last night the local elementary school was listed at the bottom of the television screen. We visited with neighbors across the street. Our neighbor wanted to show us the Australian guy who doesn't have arms or legs, and maintains hope and gratitude for life.

A lesson for us as he goes about his day. He brushes his teeth, shaves, even types. He jumps into the pool, enjoys his pet dog and travels the world giving hope to humanity. A wonderful lesson from my neighbor's computer screen. He has the Zig Ziglar attitude at the young age of twenty three. He isn't limited by his physical limitations. A lesson for all who take this wintry day a bit slower, a routine stopped for most, even the fully functioning among us.

Day four of a winter storm which leaves many stranded, alone at home, inside protected from the elements. Two days ago, even the mailman didn't make it through. Yesterday the box was full of Christmas cards alongside regular business mail.

One Christmas letter wrote from the home's perspective. In other words who lives there? Who visits? Who drops by for their very first time? As it works out, it is a loud new grandchild, a first for the house and those who occupy a once quiet home. Maybe my older sister doesn't need Julia's writing manual?

There are pictures along with the cards. A time once a year to reconnect with people close by and at a distance. We write what happens in our year, they share parts of what happens in theirs. Today much of the neighborhood is quiet. Midday people venture outside, some sled, others just enjoy the snow. The snow's glitter contrasts the more common rain and dark of a typical Pacific Northwest winter.

Madeline helps edit more of my book on the Tenderloin. She enjoys the character sketches of the people who lived in the Tenderloin years ago. People who were once part of my daily routine; I'd gotten to know many, seeing them day to day.

Today we are once again snow bound, marooned inside. The kids played school yesterday, their webkins playing alongside. The telephone just rang; our friend in London wants to hear of our local winter wonderland. No snow in London, rather the dark dreary British winter. We note a few more Christmas cards must be finished up, written and placed in the outgoing mail.

Money magazine was in yesterday's mail. The managing editor leaves. This month's issue is thinner. They had the lead story for much of the past year and a half. I wonder if they got the economic story right, perhaps that is why this edition is thinner.

It's a thin story to write. Still it doesn't right itself, most would prefer to erase 2008. Fewer are expressing what they know for sure, on the financial front. The past year changes a few rules, maybe even common held assumptions.

We write of the furnace kicking on, lately it runs more often to offset the low temperatures outside. A polar bear sits across my desk. He came in a Christmas card yesterday from a local property management company. He sits among a snow bank with silver stars lining the card's edge.

"Happy Holidays," the card reads. A time of year to write those we think of often, yet realistically connect with once a year, via the annual Christmas letter. Others sit beside us ongoing, some days we take time to notice them. We write thinking we use our words, maybe they have a hand in stories which write themselves.

Though a thaw outside, the garbage recyclers called late last night warning they may not be available in the morning for their routine Thursday pickup. Today the snow melts, the kids remain off school, the fourth day due to winter weather.

Still today it is calm before the storm. By four this afternoon the freezing temperatures will be back, back changing the wintry landscape for all. Ice keeps most none essentials at a stand still.

A plane flies in the distance. People travel this time of year to reunite with family and friends. The annual Christmas cards suffice for the rest of us. We write of how our lives progress, the places we visit, the daily routine. We might even pass on a book which was once recommended to us.

Each year our cards get more clever. Some write from their home's viewpoint, others in the voice of their pet. It keeps the letter crisp in case there are fewer details to add excitement to our past year narrative. Much like talking about the weather, still the forecasters get today wrong, not even close.

Another plane climbs in the sky. Late in getting my morning writing done and thus it is a different schedule for the outside distractions. Inside all are asleep. Melissa doesn't have to call the office before she leaves this morning. Yesterday she left work early, so too for the day before. This weather changes by the hour, depending on just a few degrees whether we get snow, hail or rain, sometimes a mix of all three.

The snow has brightened up an otherwise dark and dreary time of year. The Christmas wreath is attached to the front door. My brother in Philadelphia gives many in the family a wreath made from a mission in West Virginia. The money goes to a good cause.

Last night the Secret Millionaire went to Shenandoah Pennsylvania. It once thrived, not so much today. The mother and daughter team follow a few locals, before deciding who to help out. One, a nurse who struggles to make ends meet after losing her husband to a heart attack. Another helps by running a local daycare; a daycare mixed with foster care alongside raising her own children.

The last one operates a beauty parlor. She delivers food to the poor in her spare time. She drops a filled box at various porches, trying to reach the whole neighborhood over time. The Secret Millionaire is most touched by the hair dresser's effort, thus she receives the largest gift.

This gift passed on so others will have food. This in America 2008. How can we as a country get this wrong? Prosperous America with whole neighborhoods in despair. Makes the weather forecasters effort at accuracy insignificant, irrelevant especially this holiday season.

Today the kids are off school. Snow and ice give them an extra week's recess during their otherwise two week Christmas break. Snow lines the street; garbage cans line the snow. They will give it a second attempt to collect our week's debris today. If not, then we are to place the recyclables on next week's regular schedule.

Schools, garbage collectors, all of our schedules affected by the week of snow. Our schedules rearranged, rescheduled. The kids made a snowman in the backyard before lunch yesterday. Later they played school, keeping themselves entertained. Late afternoon Madeline and I read more of life in the Tenderloin. She likes the character sketches of people met within the depressed area amid otherwise thriving San Francisco.

We write of the people met, those who meet us. We write of what we read and those books we pass on to others. The Christmas cards continue to stream in. Two Federal Express packages came in yesterday from New York. A card from friends now in Reno, my wife Melissa worked at their eye clinic during high school back in Anchorage.

Christmas, a time of year to hear from people at a distance. People often heard from once a year, although years ago they were part of our daily life. This book on the Tenderloin recaptures some of those moments.

Those people who are in the residential hotel lobby the five days a week I worked there. Madeline especially enjoys meeting them within the book's chapters. Even years later, they are fresh in memory, similar to the details of our loved ones final departure, unbeknownst to us at the time. They wave and we think they are just being overly enthusiastic. Maybe they know something which takes us thirty five years to piece together.

The concurrent story is biographical and Madeline is already familiar with most of that storyline. Thus she looks forward to meeting more of the new characters, the Tenderloin hotel residents. Later in the book she will meet her aunt, the one missing in the M&M picture taken earlier this summer.

Last night the Secret Millionaire spent time in North Las Vegas. Even with its blanket of snow it's hard to cover up this urban blight. He helps a quadriplegic start a wheelchair business, and later a woman feed more of the locals. His family donation goes toward funding a building for homeless children. A place of refuge, food, shelter and providing computers to further their job search.

He is a changed person after seeing the other side of town. He's been to Las Vegas often, bypassing this section of town, not knowing it exists, same for the Tenderloin for too many tourists and residents alike.

Christmas cards continue to stream in. One mentions they received their first grandchild this year. Another says the same. Still another says they are in the process of selling the family home. There aren't many takers in this real estate market, meanwhile they've moved into their new retirement condominium along a golf course.

The tone of the Christmas letter matches how many feel at year end. People no longer lose tens of thousands, many feel shortchanged, our homes down in value, our retirement accounts less than half their value from the beginning of the year. Still we contribute and second guess our investment decisions.

There is little profit left in Happy Valley, once a desirable neighborhood. Five years ago our demographics were enviable, today not so much. Same for the United States. Once we led, today some would suggest we are no longer competitive.

Regrettable, we fought in Iraq to save another country, and left much of our own in shambles. Fewer trust in the government systems and safeguards. Each day brings more news of financial scandal, political scandal.

Regrettable in the United States as we begin 2009, much of the middle class has collapsed. Thus they cash out their retirements; they sell off the family home. They write Christmas letters; letters without a sense of hope within their lines of how the past year played out.

There is despair, regret and fear. People are furious with the state of affairs. Bailouts amid a collapse of our political, economic and most any other system people once trusted. Even the currency, the United States dollar is diluted, with each bailout becoming worth less and less. The Christmas cards continue to come in, fewer in an upbeat festive mood. Truly there is less to celebrate as we close out the year that was 2008.

This morning there is an accumulation of snow. It snowed yesterday; it snowed for much of the week. It will snow for much of the coming week. Snow in Las Vegas, even New Orleans is strange weather indeed. Still Portland does not get weeks of snow, or an accumulation of snow for that matter. We will have a white Christmas this year.

Much of the country is blanketed with a storm full of snow. Airport delays, local traffic delays, Portland metropolitan roads required all drivers to have chains before yesterday ended. In other words stay off the roads, stay home. Neighbors came over for a game of Farkle and a bowl of chili. Madeline made the corn bread. The kids also helped make the chocolate fudge. The coffee is brewing, maybe a piece of fudge would go well in awakening us on this snowed in day.

Writing opens ears, we are more apt to hear the twist of phrase, the unusual wording and jot it down before we forget. Forget the funny sentence, or more apt to forget how it was worded in the first place. Often kids have a way of saying things adults would phrase differently.

Yesterday my daughter Abby said "Don't end your song." She meant continue playing the piano until the neighbors show up for the dice game and chili. Adults sometimes also phrase it differently. A job application asks "How did you fix the fail?"

I spent part of yesterday looking at property on line. Maui, overpriced Maui, still even their prices have come down. Eight hundred thousand dollars buys a small two bedroom condominium in its Wailea neighborhood - a lottery win for most of us.

Ft Lauderdale Florida has been featured lately as a place for real estate bargains. A two thousand square foot townhouse for one hundred seventy thousand dollars. Another, a two bedroom, two bath condominium for merely one hundred seven thousand dollars. A bargain considering its location and amenities, let alone it comes furnished.

Florida has trouble unloading its second home ownership market. Arizona has similar bargains. The thirty year fixed mortgages hit a low, below five percent this past week, which should move inventory.

Two more Christmas cards are in the mail. One from my nephew in upstate New York. He will marry later in July. Another from an army friend who is content. Her word and I believe her. Three grandchildren keep her busy. Lucky grandchildren, as I've kept in touch with my army friend thirty years.

Christmas a time to say hello to friends we connect with once a year. We don't see each other as often with the passage of time. Years ago the telephone rang; our Christmas card to a longtime friend had been opened by the executor of the estate.

Our friend had passed away. Wanda was no longer with us at year end. Wanda who once remarked on her sibling within.

The initial write up of our Christmas letter went something along the line of our neighbors saying we have our health, homes, and jobs, not everyone can say this at year end. Luckily we edited a second and third edition before mailing. Then again the wording is accurate as it works out. For Wanda, one uncle and two aunts who also passed away this year. Even more lost their homes in foreclosure, to say nothing of the dwindling job market.

A blanket of snow covers everything outside, snow and ice, a foot and a half of snow and ice. Between the two, many trees twist out of shape, and we hope spring back once the weather warms. It snowed for seven days now. Maybe no big deal in the upper tier of the country, still this is unusual for Portland.

A winter wonderland people tire of soon enough. Everything is at a standstill. Already the Christmas break for school children. Most nonessential work is cancelled for tomorrow as well. No daily newspaper yesterday. It definitely will not be around today with the extra eight inches of snow, ice on top.

Snow I log in on my calendar, the seventh time in as many days. 2008 one for the record book, now we will add this winter storm to the list of records. Interstate 84, the main road leading east, is closed. Surely by day two, the backlog of traffic builds, each impatient with their eighteen wheelers waiting to head east, or maybe return east.

The kids sleep in. Yesterday they played outside briefly as it's too cold, cold and slippery. Later we watched two movies as my wife baked. Today we will eat more banana bread, fudge along with a hot beverage. Still it is turning out to be a miserable shopping season for retailers, even before the foot and a half of snow, ice on top and within. Another holiday season without our friend Wanda.

I usually write in on my calendar the days it snows. They are rare enough in the Portland metropolitan area. This year it's been logged in eight days in a row. Snow is no longer something rare to note on our calendars, this year it's a daily occurrence. So far a forty year record, surely the record will be expanded before this winter storm is over.

Again today the city shuts down. A second day in a row without mail, the whole east side of Portland didn't get a delivery yesterday. The mailman missed a day last week. Garbage routines go by the wayside. The airport, port and bus station at a standstill. Delays and cancellations rule the day. Yesterday, two thirds of Portland city buses were offline.

That kind of winter. The kids sleep in, Melissa too. Last night we watched movies and had dinner with neighbors. Earlier another neighbor asked if we need anything from the grocery store. A turkey dinner would be nice for Christmas. Still it is days away and anything can happen before then. Another neighbor does a Costco run. Costco has trouble keeping their shelves stocked. They are out of lasagna, and we take the last loaves of garlic bread.

People are house bound locally, across the country it is a wintry mix. Albany, New York breaks over one hundred year records. Cold and lots of snow for much of the country. We write about the weather and getting out of the weather, shoveling a path to the outside world. People don't like being stranded, isolated. Faith builds community; doubt on the other hand wears it down. Relationship and community is a good thing.

The kids play outside as I break away some of the ice and shovel a path from the garage to the street. I clear away the sidewalk, the one buried again from a new day's ten inches of fresh snow. We will have a white Christmas. The lights blinked last night, just long enough to require resetting clocks.

Fortunately, we have not lost electricity for any length of time. Much of the landscape, trees, shrubs and ground cover buried in inches of snow and ice. I hope they spring back once the weight melts away. Like us, they bounce back after an abrupt additional weight. Sometimes it includes the news of our loved ones passing.

We write in the early morning calm. We note the furnace runs more frequently to keep up with the cold outside, a day before Christmas Eve. An unusual winter wonderland leaves many wondering what's next?

Chains are required on metropolitan streets, suppose if it's not critical, stay off the roads. Most can't reach the main roads to go anywhere. Most businesses are closed. No business again today, not an ideal way to run a profitable venture.

Christmas Eve and we are left with snow banks, ice and a few day old newspapers. Day eleven for those counting snow days. Day three for the days missed by the mailman. The post office delivers in spite of the weather, perhaps it is part of the change promised.

I clear part of a neighbor's driveway, sidewalk and front doorstep. I find their front door buried within the two feet of snow. The phone answering machine catches a few messages while I shovel outside. A coworker says she will not be in tomorrow. She can't get inside her house without a half hour of shoveling, thus she spends the night at her parents. Another leaves a message the gift exchange this year will be a New Years gift exchange, although they shopped early and have presents to deliver.

Local retailers lose their best holiday shopping days this year due to weather. The economy had already slowed business. The late December storm among the worst on record for Portland, leaves many retailers empty handed. Surely many restaurants also suffer the lack of business. It will be a white Christmas. Last year it merely snowed on Christmas day, this year many are inundated with two feet of snow, with more falling.

It has brightened up the Northwest winter skies. Still many stranded at the bus station and airport aren't feeling merry. Their Christmas is spent in transit, getting there will be their holiday memory this year. We write of our day, our weather, and our answering machine messages.

We write of our over burdened landscape. Few trees and shrubs will now likely bounce back once the caked ice and snow melt. Rime, I read recently is what this caked on ice is called. Already a few roofs have collapsed, as well as trees and power lines.

Our lights blink this morning. My wife has the television on to see if the federal government is open for business. A mixed signal, they are open. The newscasters on the other hand warn to stay off the roads. Our interstate is closed other than for emergency vehicles. Carry chains, wear chains if you travel.

My wife watches a few minutes after the lights and television blink back on. She will not go to work today. Something about falling snow, two feet of snow on the unplowed streets and having to wear chains. Many won't need further incentive to spend Christmas Eve at home, warm and safe at home, in spite of the record making weather.

The clocks are reset after a third power outage. Luckily these outages are just long enough to make us reset clocks; still it is a hassle even on Christmas morning. Last night we spent time with neighbors before coming home to open presents. The tree was filled with presents even though we agreed ahead of time to cut back this year. The week of snow probably forces many to cut back, getting around in the two feet of snow with a mix of ice has been a challenge.

The clocks are reset, the Christmas tree empty of wrapped presents. The kids play with some of their new toys, Polly Pockets still a favorite as are the clothes from Aeropostale. The acoustic guitar garners a few sighs. Later we will set up the kids desks from Ikea, the ones anyone with a little time on their hands can build. I hope they go together easier than the crib from years before, which took a few hours longer than the packaging inferred.

We are going to our neighbors for a brunch. Turkey will have to wait until the day after Christmas; otherwise we would eat two big meals in the same day. Madeline just stopped in my den with a short story on butterflies. Several pages long, it ends with the words - the end. Not a bad place to end, or start.

Actually start where we are goes the advice. Start with the plane flying overhead on an early Christmas morning. The calm Christmas morning following eleven days of storm. The morning with the gift wrap scattered about, kids playing with their new toys, adults reading some of their new books or writing one of their own.

People busy with their early morning Christmas, sipping orange juice and waiting for a toast to pop before crossing the street for brunch. There we will enjoy stuffed French toast and more coffee. Abby stops into my den wondering when we will start building her desk. Let's wait until after the brunch. Why ruin a perfectly good meal?

Ideally they will be easy to build; otherwise it could take the most of an otherwise snow covered Christmas day. She is excited about her new desk. They both are excited about their new desks for their bedrooms; they saw them on display at Ikea weeks before.

Another airplane climbs in the distance. Over seven hundred flights cancelled at PDX during the past few days. Clearly some are not having Christmas go as planned. While it is a white Christmas, for many it is Christmas spent in transit, getting there instead of being there with family and friends.

Some forging new friendships along the way, their common bond, anger at the airlines and being stranded. So too for those at the train and bus stations. A white Christmas proves difficult to maneuver. A Christmas season many are forced to spend close to home, and perhaps how it's meant to be. Still another airplane flies in the distance; they make up for their delays earlier in the week.

Chapter 28

"It's not just an idea, it's a disappointment," I tell my neighbor. Finding junk in the trunk, this time a field of junk lodged underneath my kids' beds. We moved the beds to rearrange a dresser, which makes room for their desks. Christmas day is spent putting together dowels, screws, and anchor screw caps in their new Ikea desks. I hope they grow with the kids as they go through grade, middle and high school.

One is a bright red, the other oak, both with white accents and a writer board. A board easily erased once they tire of their message of the day. We have stuffed French toast, sausage, cranberry juice and coffee for a Christmas brunch with neighbors. A day later they come over for turkey, dressing and cards.

A full Christmas celebration ends with fun and games. In the meantime we locate the right piece according to an etched diagram leaving us frustrated before the final assembly dowels and screw caps are fastened.

It's early morning and the garbage and recyclables are curbside. Last week they couldn't get through the neighborhood. This week the pickup is delayed a day due to the Christmas holiday. There is more to recycle this time of year, wrapping paper, cardboard, and turkey remains.

The mailbox will probably be filled as the mailman missed the past four days. Maybe the Harry and David food tower will also get here. Their delivery is late. They will receive a telephone call; something was amiss with this order. Not the best advertisement for mail order gifts, on time delivery matters.

It's quiet outside, the two feet of snow is slow in melting. A few vehicles are parked, buried under record Portland snow, record amount for the month of December. It snows on Christmas day, last year it snowed as well. A white Christmas keeps many close to home, in their neighborhood most likely.

Some build gifts for their kids; others enjoy board games, or a game of cards. Still others eat stuffed French toast, sausage, turkey and stuffing. Eating desserts of every variety passing Christmas day which leaves many snowed in. Some find unwanted treats underneath their kids' beds, rearranging the furniture on Christmas day.

The snow melts outside; a steady rain helps it disintegrate. Parts of the street are down to pavement, as are parts of the sidewalk covered the past two weeks with daily snow and ice. We write what is atop our desk and what is outside our window. The evergreen sprayed in the family room to give the essence of a real Christmas tree permeates my den. It smells like Christmas. The evergreen outside my den window drops its load of snow and springs back to life.

For days its branches extend horizontal with the added weight of snow and ice. Part of it lodges on the house gutters, preventing the evergreen from stretching further. The rain continues to fall. A whiff of evergreen floats into my den, onto my writing paper.

A Christmas list is atop my desk. On construction paper, it records who we will later thank this holiday season. Several give gift cards, one for a bookstore, another for a coffee treat along the route.

Melissa receives a CD titled The Secret. We watched it last night with a neighbor. Our clothes dryer didn't turn on after a recent power outage, or more to the point, after a power surge. Our neighbor lost her refrigerator days later after another blink in electricity.

That's the consensus as to the run in appliance failures. Another neighbor waits for the dishwasher repair man. The Secret video has us believe we literally attract this to our households.

Whatever we ask for and believe we receive. The law of attraction, like electricity, we don't have to understand to use. Like our broken appliances few understand, three of us in the neighborhood not able to use. So it goes life simply applies the law of attraction. Ask to write a book and next thing a pen is in hand writing page after page.

Other days a book falls in our lap meant to be read. Then there are those days we read of ourselves inside the middle of a book. It happens.

Still whatever we want life provides, there for the asking, the believing says the video. The believing part is what short circuits most. We don't feel worthy, deserving, thus we place minimal orders from the universal catalog. Know there is more than enough to go around.

On a lighter side of appliance breakdowns, we rush to eat food before it spoils. Sometimes it includes a frittata with avocado, onion, mushrooms, cheese, zucchini and of course egg. A few beverages are placed outside in the snow, a record snow for parts of the otherwise mild Pacific Northwest.

The furnace runs although it is already forty degrees outside. We write what is going on outside, inside our homes and within our thoughts. Beyond our thoughts attracting what we once envisioned for ourselves. Receiving whatever we ask and believe the universe provides, even words for some.

The Sunday newspaper is outside. The snow melts, maybe this week will return to normal. The past three have been unusual. Instead of the holiday rush of excitement, we wait to see if there is activity outside, specifically will there be a full work day? Will the daily newspaper get delivered? The mailman missed our neighborhood six times in as many days. The garbage is now two weeks behind schedule.

Much of the landscape is battered, regrettably our new subdivision was just benefiting from a wide variety of trees, shrubs, and bushes. The ice ruins many; we will prune back the damage and replant this spring.

2009 a new year, a year of replanting. A new administration comes to Washington, one promising change. Some of the people haven't changed and few doubt things will remain as they have always been. Still a country's policies don't always change with the change in personalities.

It's quiet outside, no traffic, planes or even birds. Inside is equally quiet as the house sleeps in. Christmas vacation for the kids and they stay up later than usual, sleep in later than usual. Vacation takes us out of routine, off schedule. So too for the wintry mix of weather the past two weeks.

We write of our daily experience, including the times we slide our way out the neighborhood to the nearby mall. A mall filled with people happy to leave their homes. The wintry weather left most stranded the past two weeks. We stop in at Sears and leave with a clothes dryer.

Perhaps a power surge ruined our ten year old model. We also buy a few new pans and a griddle, now the economy has us eating at home. Still we stop at Red Robin to celebrate a neighbor's fortieth birthday. We celebrate with friends, burgers, and ice tea. We celebrate amid the snow melt, amid the steady stream of rain. Restaurant meals once again reserved for special occasions.

Just now the rain picks up; it melts the last two feet of snow. Flooding is a possibility in lower lying areas. Being able to drive away without fear of slippery roads or shoveling snow is a luxury for much of the upper section of the United States mid winter. The Pacific Northwest gets lots of rain, while much of the country accumulates snow. We aren't equipped to remove the snow and ice, thus it stalls the everyday. The lack of mail, morning paper, even garbage service breaks our routine.

The mailbox now fills with cards after a break in service. A box of cookies and a few pictures are also in the mix. One a family photograph, another a high school senior portrait. There are several Christmas letters too. Still we wait for the Harry and David Christmas food pyramid.

Those perishable fruits are somewhere along the route. My wife sends them a note regarding their holiday delivery record. Someone's Christmas gift held up three days after the holiday and counting. The rain continues.

The rain falls outside as we begin the final week of 2008. Another year end approaches. For 2008, it isn't fast enough for investors. Some years stand out more than others, this is one few will forget.

It changes many lives financially; it also took three family members and brings us a new one, baby Nixon. The rains wash away two weeks of record snow for the Portland area. Initially exciting, clean and white, it soon becomes an ice heap to shovel. Later the road sand mixes in making a gray slush, some of which remains on our cars.

The daily newspaper is back in our driveway. The mailman will resume his schedule. They missed six days this December. 2008 a year of records, not all good. My desk crowded before the holiday now clutters with more notes, photographs and Christmas reminders. We write within the mix atop our desk and within the final calendar week of the year. A routine week and yet there are deadlines unique to the end of a year.

My college roommate writes, sending a card with a calendar attached. In college, I'd given a speech on the indispensability of everyday calendars. I opened with - Each of us has one. I find three without searching my room continued the second line. Apparently my roommate never forgot that funny speech.

Neither have I. The assignment was to catch the audience's attention early on and keep their attention throughout the speech. I practiced it many times in front of my roommate and apparently it still holds his attention, as we both get a recycled laugh twenty five years later.

Can only wonder what he'll say once I share I've written a book, a book or three? He'll probably wonder if I mention him. Never know how a gift will be received, so too for books.

Some don't react the way we would expect. Rather than genuine excitement for our venture, they are hesitant, even puzzled by our writing. Writers don't write for others, we primarily write for ourselves. It is where the satisfaction and art of writing are found. Still if others enjoy our words, that is always a bonus, even those bestsellers or special books we pass on which resonate with us.

We write in the early morning rain, the days following the Christmas celebrations, the days ending the current year. We write of our daily routine and those planes heard in the distance. We write as the shadow of our writing hand moves across the page, the shadow leaving a word trail behind.

A few Christmas lights hang from neighboring homes. They are in stark contrast to the usual Pacific Northwest winter darkness. The snow no longer available to bounce off their color, their light. The polar bear sits on my desk. It sits on a mound of snow as if posing for the camera. It's a white fur ball looking directly at us, as it lounges in the snow.

Two neighbors leave for work, a work week abbreviated due to the holidays. We will have breakfast with friends and then spend a night at the coast. Many hotel rooms remain vacant even during the holiday season, not a good year for the hospitality business. Perhaps not a good year for business itself.

Before our trip to the beach the new clothes dryer gets delivered. It is an unexpected Christmas gift, one presented at the last minute. We will never know if the appliance ran its useful life, or it stopped working due to a power surge.

The recent snow and ice had our lights blinking often. No long periods of lost power, still power surges are never a good thing. Several neighbors have problems with their appliances. One an expensive refrigerator, another dishwasher trouble, not good timing amid the otherwise busy holiday season.

Yesterday the mailman didn't go by. Odd to think the mail doesn't get delivered. It's been seven times during the past few weeks. Yesterday there was bare pavement, so one wonders what goes on with the postal service? Our gift basket from Harry and David has yet to arrive as well.

We had a winter storm mid month, suppose it will take weeks before everything returns to routine. They had closed the main freeway going east from Portland. The airport cancelled over seven hundred flights during the mid December winter storm.

Many spend their holidays in transit. They will have more to write about in next year's Christmas letter. It adds a chapter to our book. All travel has this potential, even the travel which goes as planned.

Sometimes the most memorable moments are those which take on a life of their own - they write themselves. The delay at JFK airport ends with an Amtrak ride for the final leg of the trip. Waiting three hours for a casino shuttle running every twenty minutes. The purple bus in Las Vegas, the "You can't miss it" one in Las Vegas mid July.

There is always something to write if we'll just make ourselves available to log it in. The airport delay, the sidelined shuttle, the people met waiting alongside us. Even those who passed on all those years before, they too wait alongside with us.

Writing takes the time to notice what goes on around us. The music from our nearby radio, the plane in the distance, the kids sleeping, our spouse who stops in our den before heading out for groceries. Think my wife might have meant a stop at Starbucks as she received a gift card again this year.

We use our gift cards the week after Christmas, some save them for a month or three. They are a treat, regardless when we cash them in. We write of our everyday and those moments which don't go as planned or expected. We write of life's surprises and its timely treasures. Sometimes it is a book we decide to read or one recommended by others. Or surprise ourselves and write one of our own.

The front entryway light is on. Sears will deliver the new dryer within a two hour window. An early window so I'm up as the rest of the house sleeps in this last day of 2008. "Alleluia!" say all too many. We write in the early morning of the planes flying by and what we wait around for. Sometimes it's a new dryer; other times a neighbor's visit. We will see neighbors later today to celebrate the yearend.

A Christmas card from a former boss was in yesterday's mail. We met on a job in New York City many years ago. Later we both moved to San Francisco, before settling elsewhere. I move to Portland, he settles in Denver.

We write of what's atop our desks and what is on our schedule. I load up on ink as both printers signal to replace their ink cartridges. I also stop in at Goodwill, leaving with two books. One on teaching ourselves to sing, the other on reaching targets.

Singing is natural enough, the trouble begins when we force ourselves or breathe improperly. Standing helps too, it helps our best voice sing. The other book suggests the win or lose of goals is a bad thing. Shoot for targets instead, keep shooting regardless if we hit the bull's eye. Thus targets are more accommodating, encouraging, and flexible.

The Goodwill parking lot was full. Many look for bargains this year, this time of year. There are racks of books waiting to be browsed and ultimately purchased. I have a gift card to Barnes & Noble. I will use it later in the year.

Most likely will purchase a journal as I've kept several, jotting down trivia, overheard comments, quotes and anything else I may want to recall. I jot it down in a journal and later reread these notes, quotes and pieces of information.

Sometimes it's on how to better use our singing voice, or reaching personal targets. Other times on how we go about writing, what is behind our writing? What is beyond all art? Most would agree the doing is art itself. The process as important as the finished product. So too with writing, if not life.

Many are so focused on the end, the goal we forget to appreciate the journey. One example refers to people climbing poles in Maui. They are so focused on the climb; they fail to take in the splendor of the Hawaiian island from their perch high atop the training pole.

It happens. We get caught up in the scheduling of our days; we have deadlines and goals to achieve. We have delivery people to meet. We wait for and on others, often we neglect to take time for ourselves, our own growth, or writing. Instead we rush through, reading other's words and waiting on their timelines.

We have a choice whether to hear those distant planes or concentrate on our own tasks at hand. Know we are doing the right thing at the right time. In other words, we are where we are meant to be, doing what we are meant to be doing. Some days it's waiting for a clothes dryer delivery, or saying farewell to an ugly year.

It's a downpour outside, the wind gusts on occasion. The furnace kicks on amid the outside noise. Two weeks of snow is now followed by days of rain, heavy rain. The skies sad to leave behind a year which dropped investments by over thirty five percent. That's ugly enough. Still one has to add the government bailouts to the mix.

Stir it together and 2008 is one for the economic record books. Fortunately the year of financial change is over.

Now it rains outside, the first day of the new year. Perhaps it waters down a new crop, a new growth in altogether new directions. Onward and upward, the future looks bright as there need not be much improvement for it to look like staggering growth. Opportunity is just around the corner, prosperity for the United States and world; a world mired in recession.

All cycles end and thus this year too may be one for the record books. Politically the landscape changes after eight years of one administration. Many feel the outgoing President's downfall is the handling of Hurricane Katrina. Natural disasters take on a life of their own; regrettably it took many human lives along with the physical devastation. One of my sisters experiences this storm first hand. The rest of the family learns of her vacation mid storm. It too writes a story.

Chapter 29

————— ⋅❦⋅ —————

Stories are penciled in ongoing. Inside the middle, start there and then return to introduce and later conclude what we have written. Some days it's simple, we write what we've read, imagined, or maybe lived which seems fiction at this point, foreign to our life today. Still we must add those characters and include ourselves in the mix to write our books.

I spent the day rereading parts of this book. I wanted it to be written from the Tenderloin hotel lobby group. My wife said their voice could not work, it wouldn't be credible.

Fiction takes us alongside the writer. Still it has to be credible, if only a make believe world. "How could they possibly know current events?" she asks, "let alone the day to day routine of elementary and middle school aged children." Make it up, I argued.

I'll save their voice for another book. "It is too personal to be written by another," my wife says "much less written by a group of others." Does this mean fiction is one person working alone? One person at a time creates a made up world? Sometimes it helps to write alone only later share our stories, words and settings with others. With each edit our story gets better, if not told with fewer words.

Today I set aside another one hundred pages of daily writing. I'll read through in search of a story within. Read some write novels in one month. Perhaps they do, yet how much longer do they spend with the edit process?

This particular book has been written awhile. Still the editing continues. With each reread we find sections which don't add to the story. Ideally one day we reach the point when we are left with story only, regardless how the story is later classified.

It too is a point of dissention. "Fiction can't be true," my wife continues. "Those things happened to you, thus you can't paint them as fiction." Ask the reader in Nebraska? I reply. To them, it is fiction, they don't know my story; or more apt, aren't in the middle of it, the day to day and a Vermont summer long ago.

Writing is difficult when considering the various timeframes and who our audience includes. With the internet, our words might be read worldwide and many years later. A timeframe may not work yet becomes irrelevant decades later. If the lobby group wants to write a story, have at it. Still, I will wait for another book to let them further their story.

While there may be rules, art doesn't necessarily follow them. Paintings happen. Music plays itself. Those moments happen by happenstance, say painters and songwriters. After awhile the artist stops and frames what he has.

Perhaps writing is much the same. We stop at an interesting place, assuming we have reached interesting places along the way and take our reader alongside. Never leave the reader behind, especially if it's your wife as second reader. They'll invariably ask, "Who's telling this story?"

Words tell a story, so too for people in the story, those who write it, those who live it, and those who later come along and read about it. Words and their people tell a story whether in a Tenderloin residential hotel lobby, within family, a group Bible study, or even us as we walk through our neighborhood within our own thoughts.

Writing echoes our voice. We use details from our life to write our own story. Sometimes we use details from our life to write the story of others, the story of humanity reflected within those details. All of them, even those twenty pages which ultimately refocus, if not define life.

Many stories hint of God, or an interconnection within our universe. He is there whether we write about him or not. He is reflected in our stories and most likely prefers we include details of his life within the mix.

That writing stirs, moves, and gives our writing voice, perhaps an echo from those who touch us along the way. Even those who once asked us as kids "What do you plan to do with your life?" We write so others can read along with our story and ideally hear more of their own.

Books do this on occasion; the better ones do it every time. We read of ourselves, our life echoed in the detail, our voice echoed in the writing. Each of us has one, a story filled with laughter, tears, activity and relationship.

Each of us has one, a story or three. We tell them we are working on it, placing words on the page is the least of it. Our book has already been written, now we just have to get through words. Varied as the details may be, they make us who we are, and write our books. Rather than a notation on a calendar, they fill our books; tell our story one setting, one sibling at a time.

Where do we start to write a book held inside us, a book we carry through the years? Inside the middle? It's difficult to write a story without placing parts of our own selves within those words. Last week I was at Costco. Abby was sick, home for part of a second week away from school. She has been under the weather since three classmates at her group table were sick weeks before.

We are at Costco to buy paper towels, vegetable oil and dishwasher soap. I look through the books before leaving with the ongoing staples. One book I want sells for eight dollars and fifty cents. My third grade daughter Abby chimes in she often buys her books for eleven dollars, sometimes more.

I shop the Goodwill shelves and find bargains there. I leave the recent bestseller on the Costco table. Later that night at a weekly Bible study, the group leader has a stack of this particular book on her desk at the front of the room.

There it is again and so I figure this recent bestseller is meant to be read. I buy it and trust the Bible study leader's life has been enhanced by this particular book. She has raved about it for several weeks. It is written by someone in Gresham and we lived in that Portland suburb for much of the 1990's.

It's a picturesque town with an older section, its downtown core. There are boulevards with most every modern day convenience and franchise leading out of town. This bestseller starts just beyond Gresham. It takes us to Multnomah Falls, stops in for lunch at Hood River and then drives along the Columbia River Gorge to eastern Oregon. Much of the book centers on Wallowa Lake in the mountains on the east side of the state.

Early on a military colored vehicle leaves the campground with a six year old and her red dress visible from the passenger seat. This bestseller is difficult, it hits home. Twice. I'm told to get through the first third of the book and then it gets better - a page turner. Suppose skipping pages thirty through fifty in each of our lives would have made life easier. Still those pages make, even define life, they write our books.

I e-mail my friend Chris I wrote a book on how people come and go in our lives, still others never leave. Like reading this latest bestseller, sometimes it's painful getting through the words. In my case it's not campsite abduction, still the young sibling disappears in the blink of an eye.

Rather than leave in an olive green vehicle with a red dress flapping in the windshield, my sister waves as she rounds the bend in the road. She is in a late 1960's model Ford truck, red with a white grill.

Exactly like the one my third grade daughter Abby sees on her digital camera. I don't tell her why I took the photograph. She asks as she scans through her camera's pictures. I too ask when this truck stops me in my tracks as I walked through our neighborhood recently. Thirty five years later its grill stops me in my tracks.

It's comforting to think they are beside us as we live life, write our books, walk through the neighborhood, or e-mail friends. Still the day they leave in a blink of an eye is something we never forget. It not only writes our books, it colors how we read others. Even bestsellers might affect us differently than the author intends. Still Linda has that book stacked, front and center for each of us to read.

The telephone is busy this morning. First, a car warranty reminder, then a telemarketer on how to reduce credit card debt. Just now my wife Melissa calls - Abby has an infection and would be home in forty five minutes. They will stop at the pharmacy first.

An earlier call was from Melissa's coworker wondering where she is. Although we don't say they will be in later, instead we run upstairs and pray they return. We hope someone has the story wrong. There must be something missing among the details, people don't just leave. Or do they?

Still having a five year old sibling leave without warning is sad, even if we have a dozen other siblings. Three to a bed, as it were. Sometimes three in the front, three in the back and yes, three in the trunk.

Life in Vermont all those years ago went something like this. A rope with a tire hanging from a branch and kids fighting for their chance for a swing. Bucolic, a bucolic early ride through life.

Funny most people have this first impression of life among a large family. Like in Austria where music plays in the wind, large families are full of song. Or so, many think. Maybe it was early on.

I'm in the middle where stories start, somewhere in the middle. Robert Frost thought there were only middles. Life like books perhaps does start in the middle, and then each passing day gets better with the turn of a calendar page.

My sister waves as she rounds the bend in the road. At age five, two days after her birthday, she wears her yellow polka-dotted hat. An oversized hat which probably adds to her danger later in the day.

I refuse to go along for the ride, preferring to stay home and finish lunch. In the bestseller, a sister spends much of life second guessing her actions. Would things have turned our differently had she more carefully watched her younger sister?

Still there is a sibling within us who writes our books, if not only shadows our lives -their echo lingers. Our Bible study leader Linda says this latest best selling book "needs to be read," it's that good. Setting is what pulls in the reader. I enjoy seeing parts of Oregon within the pages, Oregon, home for the second half of my life. Yet, what happens in those early pages of our story fill the later pages, and define life going forward.

Austria is Madeline's assigned country for sixth grade. It's home to Arnold Schwarzenegger, "Silent Night" and The Sound of Music. Also home to many famous composers and psychologists. The father of Genetics is also from Austria. Freud, an Austrian himself said early childhood experiences color each of our later lives.

I find the bestseller by the Gresham author dark. The narrative is sad. While it has excellent points on forgiveness and living from a place of love, the story is hard to read. It hits home. We spent the day at Wallowa Lake after seeing my mother in law one last time. We didn't know this would be our last time.

Read all about it in my book, Postcards Found Within. Maybe I'll title it A Postcard in the Wind. Or even Twice Found Postcards. People ask how long it takes to write. Books are written over breakfast. Some take decades. All require a lifetime if we are honest.

Reading the recent bestseller brought back life in the early 1970's in Vermont. This setting is backdrop to the early years. It writes my book. It is the setting I e-mail my New York City friend about. I hadn't put the story to the page, although the book has been written for some time. It gets interrupted by the daily telephone calls, an occasional bestseller and of course e-mail; e-mail a story started by one, finished by others.

Suppose it is easier this way, some stories are painful to get through. Thus a bestseller is written, when one is able to share their story. Not the peripheral books written ongoing, rather the one book in each of us. The story, pages thirty through fifty which tell our story. The part which defines our life, writes our book. The one our friends e-mail and want to hear more. The one which resonates with them, in a way it is their story too.

The details are uniquely ours, yet the storyline goes along a similar vein, a familiar vein. In the recent bestseller, a child goes missing. In my book, she doesn't go missing; we know exactly where she is. Early on we know the consequences of a load of logs holding her down in a sawmill pond.

She is there, by our side, as we work, as we read of others pain.

Sometimes that pain is a bestseller and a friend inadvertently gives us a copy and says this "needs to be read," it's that good. If they only knew what we read as we make our way through pages thirty to fifty. In reality the entire book is hard to follow as we are brought back to our own version of events.

Still those are the best books, filled with what we tell ourselves as we read others words. Gasping at times as others relate our story. Not so much the things we tell strangers, rather strangers telling us all too familiar things. It hits home. It resonates. It's as though we read our own story.

Maybe those are in fact the best books, those reflecting our own life story within the turning pages. We continue reading the recent bestseller which touches on religion and specifically whether we see God in our everyday.

He comes to us on our worst day, and often leaves soon afterward. He hears our plea in times of crisis and is forgotten the day we leave for vacation. Still it is not God who moves.

This book goes on to say he is there beside us if only we look, listen and feel his presence. Others have written we don't write books; rather books are written through us -we hold the pen. Maybe, yet I often wish we could skip those twenty pages early on.

Still those parts separate each of us; they give us our story to write. Our story to add, our insight into maybe how things work, how things work out for the best. Early on we question why. Why this tragedy happens? Why an innocent child?

People relate through Bible study. Sometimes book clubs implode if we meet each other too honestly. People prefer a distance and maybe reason why writing is sometimes painful. We can't help but reveal part of ourselves in our writing. Even writing about an apparent other, we color how we write of them, we bring in our early experiences, later experiences, and ongoing life of experience.

Reading a bit about Austria, they mention the Austrians continue to seek the best in food, clothing, music, literature - life. They once were on top of the world and could afford the best.

Today they are a hand mirror shaped country in the midst of Europe. Notably they are a country hard to characterize physically. They've been a melting pot from the surrounding eight countries and places further, thus there is no one distinct Austrian look. There's not even one language, as in America we each have our own accent, let alone story.

Hitchcock says to make the audience suffer as long as possible. Perhaps it helps to build suspense, still until we know where a person has been, we really can't meet them where they are today. Like Austria, we are formed by our history. True for each of us, regardless how the early parts play out, or even whether there is play early on.

Writing moves us to the present. It forces us to take in our immediate surroundings and what is happening in our life right now. Writing also lets us go back and reframe what happened before. We revisit parts of life difficult or blur the first time through. We keep the lesson, however long in coming.

The bestseller says those who are fully engaged in life have God with them ongoing. God is present in their life. There is a relationship, not so much someone's words lodged in a book. Not even the Bible can take the place of relationship.

Our individual stories stay inside us until we take the time and effort to place our words onto the page. Our stories write themselves, if only we move out of the way. Books on writing say this - often.

Thirty five years later, the loss is still there. It defines our life. It is part of our book. Even New York City can't distract what is buried within us. We can't rewrite pages thirty through fifty as it were. We would like to, often we have tried, and still life is fuller because of those parts we often wish could be glossed over.

I e-mail I wrote a book on how people who once were part of our lives never leave. Its theme resonates with many, it hit home with my friend in New York City. In the recent bestseller they are on vacation in Oregon. Their life changes because of this vacation and the subsequent abduction. The author describes the scene and those scenes leading up to it.

An otherwise normal day gets replayed often in an attempt to have it turn out different. We can't replay time. We trust this is how pages thirty through fifty are to read. So too for the first thirty and those which fill the remainder of our book.

Writing often stalls by sharing our work, our words with those who might not have our best interest at heart. Other times they wish they could pen a story of their own. I knew this story was written when my friend e-mailed back wanting to read further.

Having lost both of his parents he understands how life goes on. Ironically he doesn't have the comfort of a dozen siblings as an only child. People are to live as though loved. That was the phrasing in the recent bestseller, an interesting topic in our sometimes brutal world.

Even sharing our words, our story with twenty five year friendships is a risk. They risk knowing us better, we risk letting them know us more fully. Maybe they better understand why we were distracted all those years ago. Granted New York City is distracting in and of itself, yet I mean distracted before seeing the sights of the Big Apple. We can't write those pages within our book until years later, sometimes a lifetime later.

We read about ourselves in other's books. Those who've taken the time to see through their story, to get beyond the tragedy. Life is about relationship not so much accumulation and consumption.

Still it is a way to bury a pain, to bury a loss, to insulate and keep us distant from others. Perhaps weight keeps us distant from ourselves.

Writing tells a story, reveals a story one word, one reader at a time. Authors hope their story is read, yet they can never know how it will be received. I read along hoping after the difficult campsite part it would get better. My hope was maybe this was a book which could be shared with those who've lost someone special, especially those who lose children early on.

Instead it made me write my book. Maybe my friend Chris too could see how those who've left sometimes are right beside us. They are there; it's just some days we don't notice. Sort of like God, his presence there whether or not we recognize and acknowledge it. In crisis we cry out for him, on vacation - not so much.

Best selling books relate to other people. They relate a piece of life foreign and at once all too familiar. It hits home with us. Sometimes, twice. That's the part I initially didn't like after having read through some of the book Linda excitedly passes on to us. It is a difficult read, although filled with treasures for a book club. Stand alone ideas ideal for further book club discussion.

The storyline of loss is no doubt painful for the writer to write. It is hard for me to read. I'd already gone there, been there done that. Still it's never far from our thoughts, this book that wants to get written. Even my New York friend wants to read further. I thank him for asking to preview this story. The trouble is I've spent time writing others, instead of this more difficult one.

It explains the later chapters of our lives if only we stop long enough to write pages thirty to fifty. The loss, the hardship and eventually the lesson.

Don't lose the lesson amid the loss; otherwise it is a total loss. Writing connects us to the page. It connects us to our experience. Those days which once were our daily routines, the day we notice someone missing. We think about their whereabouts, how our future will look without them as passengers on our bicycle. Our little shadow who follows our every move, strangely enough they still watch over and maybe help write our book.

They were once part of our life, and continue to color, shadow or echo and thus we remember and can detail the campsite. Or the Vermont summer, the hayfields and the otherwise bucolic Vermont countryside most everyone envisions. How wonderful having all those siblings! They don't understand how the one sibling who leaves early on writes our story. They don't, because we spare them the details.

Then some day a friend gives us a best selling book to read. Linda doesn't know what she shares. Innocent enough, yet she will know me and perhaps others better once we discuss this recent bestseller and how it affects each of us. Hitchcock would say to tell her you were the second youngest in the story.

We identify with differing characters, this particular one spent most of her life second guessing that fateful day. Luckily in real life, we understand things happen without our full comprehension. We only write what happened and what happens next. Religion is beyond understanding, thus a leap of faith.

Life is lived one day at a time. Death on the other hand ends abruptly. Thirty five years later it may write our books, yet some deaths are more difficult than others, even decades later. They stop us in our tracks reading of other's misery. They stop us in our tracks on an otherwise innocent walk around the neighborhood.

The odds are against ever coming face to face with the vehicle which last took our loved one. We remember the details too well without having to see them from across the street. Still there it is with its load of wood no less. I stop and take in the scene, fully take in this moment.

The red Ford truck.

The white grill.

The load of wood.

Missing is my sister with the oversized yellow polka-dotted hat and her five year old hand waving. She did this years ago in everyone else's bucolic Vermont. Vermont is the Green Mountain state. Even Austria reminds my daughter Madeline of Vermont's scenery. It's a wonderful place. So is Oregon's Wallowa Lake. The author doesn't care to see the campground again, much less his earlier family stops in Hood River, or Multnomah Falls along the Columbia River Gorge.

Setting pulls in a reader and keeps a writer writing. Some days we face the Pacific Ocean, yet we look elsewhere for answers instead of watching the waves and hearing the seagulls. A bestseller takes us places, just as life freezes moments and those places. Those days don't require a calendar.

Meanwhile Abby asks why the late model red truck is on her digital camera. I don't tell her it could be the front cover of my book; the twenty pages which take us a lifetime to write even though there are many occasions to finish them. Sometimes we need the nudge from an old friend who e-mails and wants to know more. Having spent time together they already know parts of our story, yet knowing more of the early parts gives them a better grasp of our life - us.

Like Austria, people too are formed by what comes before. Reading shares of another's experience. The better stories reveal the human condition. We read of ourselves as they write details once true in their life. The details which shape, color and form how their life is lived each day going forward. Forgiveness is tucked in there, along with love, relationship, maybe even God.

My sister is with me the day I saw the red truck with its white grill as I walked my neighborhood here in Oregon. She is also with me as I read of the abductor driving in his olive green getaway truck with the child's red dress flapping in the wind.

Still she is more mobile, or maybe stationary like God, rather it is us who move about. Like Madeline's book on Austria, we are influenced by what came before. Austria was once a powerhouse and today Vienna retains some of that splendor. We continue, yet it takes awhile getting accustomed to how our loved ones fill our life. Where they fit in going forward? Sometimes we place them in books and hope others benefit from our story.

Words have power, there is energy in each one. Getting them in the right order or told in a certain way promises to tell the story. Not so much details of abduction or a drowning, rather how it influences us going forward. All good stories move beyond the difficult and tell what happens in spite of the difficulty along the route, getting beyond somber details into a fuller life awaiting each of us.

Suppose those are the best selling stories, those which move us, move us further along, or at least hold the promise to get us moving in the first place. Writers are the first readers of their books. We don't necessarily know how they will end. Some days they are shifted by an incoming e-mail, or as often by a book crossing our desk. In reality a story flows through us. Our details, yet maybe not so much our story gets told. A resonance within the words hold another's interest.

We could paint the verdant New England landscape. We could add a houseful of family, a meadow full of stones which require many hands to pick. A barn full of animals keep their humans on a rigid work schedule. We could write about this easily enough as this was life, day to day all those years before. Writing plans for the future.

Still the essence and treasure of writing is in the present. Connecting with our readers is by far the greatest reward. We talk of our past experiences and future hopes. Still what we write about in our today holds their interest. Granted we do have to fill in pages thirty through fifty as it were to tell the whole story.

We tell them ours in the hope they better understand their own, whether or not they take the time to write their words and experiences to the page. Each of us has a book inside; sharing with another is often a risk. Perhaps this is why there are shelves of fiction, the truth is painful to reveal. It hurts years later; it hurts reading of loss in someone else's book.

Even a bestseller can be dark. The narrative goes there, or maybe it must in order for us to see light by the end of its chapters. It hopes to translate into a life which is fuller, lighter for each of us. Growing by someone else's pain as it were. Still, we relate as most have lost someone special if we live long enough.

Still sometimes it takes a lifetime to fully understand through loss there is gain. We watch as the Pacific Ocean waves back. We watch mesmerized as the ocean spray catches an occasional rainbow or seagull.

In the meantime a vehicle we hope to never see again shows up around the corner from our home thirty five years later. A bestseller saying much the same as our story shows up on the bookshelves. Initially we think it too expensive, and then later someone has a stack of them a desk away.

"Here, this needs to be read," they say. No matter how we tell our story it is much the same for each of us. Those left behind are never far, we take them everyday going forward. Maybe they take themselves, placing a book in our lap, showing us the dreaded vehicle we can describe in detail without it being a sidewalk away. They show up in our books as we tell a story.

We think it is our story, in reality it is their story told through us. Our loved ones who left long ago and we hope those we meet along the route. Our book is one they want to read further. They e-mail and ask as it were. We tell them we are working on it, placing words on the page is the least of it. The book has already been written, now we just have to get through the words. Use our voice say the writing manuals.

For the latest bestseller, the setting is Wallowa Lake. For me the setting is a sawmill pond in most everyone's rustic Vermont, the place where two roads diverge in a wood. The Pacific Ocean now splashes in the distance, offering to alleviate disturbing memories.

Knowing where someone has been is the first step to knowing them better. Each day we reveal a bit more of ourselves, others reveal themselves to us. Each day as we work, learn and read beside one another. Sometimes it takes a book for others to see or hear us. Maybe a book written down, lets us see ourselves most clearly. Writing forces us to listen.

Writing not so much saying something, rather something heard and passed on. This is what I heard while writing on finding meaningful work. It is what I heard walking along Las Vegas Boulevard as I wrote about the Las Vegas that farkles.

This is what I heard as my daughter said "Don't leave without your story." It wrote a book as my neighbors vacation in Hawaii and another person I'd met outside a dental clinic celebrates his luck landing in America. He is late eighties and still counting his blessings. Listening and learning of his losses, one would think he wouldn't be smiling all these years later.

He didn't leave without his story. Pages thirty through fifty and even further along in his book are sad. A story of hardship and loss, still he enjoys and savors what he has all the more because of earlier experiences. Escaping World War II could not have been fun. Some didn't leave with their stories, much less with their lives.

Writing reflects on events, people and places. We begin to connect the literary dots. Only in hindsight are we able to better appreciate what came before, those details make us who we are, and write our books.

Initially just the difficult writing of pages thirty through fifty and then moving on to the more fulfilling parts, the parts others may enjoy reading. It's easier reading, still the difficult pages get the story written, and tell the story. Without those twenty pages, we lose the parts which uniquely define each of us.

At the same time, these parts of the story relate to others. Setting pulls us in, yet the details which happen within that setting reveal the plot. Sometimes those details are upsetting and yet it is precisely what leads people on to better days. We read about them and celebrate alongside, especially when they see, hear and live life to its fullest. Most likely they weren't doing this long before pages thirty through fifty come along.

We carry those pages with us wherever we go. Sometimes it's more painful should we come upon physical reminders. Some days it is a book we read, or an e-mail from a friend who wonders just what we write about.

Those most important to us never truly leave, they are here beside us in our everyday. Even those days when our story's second reader asks to read our book. My friend has no idea what he is asking. Then again, I think he might as my e-mail piqued his interest. I'm the ninth in the midst of a oversized family; my friend is an only child in New York City. Life in Vermont, crowded amid family could not have been more opposite.

Still those parts define us, and maybe by relating the often better forgotten details we share more of ourselves. Suppose the best books do, we share ourselves, hoping something within the storyline resonates with the reader. Like a long lost loved one, our story stays with them long after they close the book. Long after they read through the difficult passages within pages thirty through fifty.

With e-mail and every day conversation we tend to by pass this part. We stay a bit distant. Through Bible study we share our faith and our personal lives. Looking through the digital camera pictures, I hesitate to tell Abby just why I took the photograph. It stopped my walk.

It takes a lifetime to better understand those life defining moments. They are still beside us, although not physically on our bicycle ready to take another tumble in a Vermont meadow. Writing reminds how life plays out.

We have a broader window in which to frame events. Reading lets us appreciate more of what we have, whether we read others' words or take the time to write our own. Words that define our life, and the day we own our words, even the difficult ones to write within pages thirty through fifty.

Chapter 30

The casino shuttle bus just left the hotel, Siletz bay is in the distance. The sun shines bright, even brighter after a day which leaves several inches of rain behind. It hit the windshield the entire two hour drive to the coast. Rivers flow fast and murky, some carry logs and other debris.

This morning many roads are closed due to flooding. A beautiful day at the beach after yesterday's cloud burst. Mid afternoon felt like evening, dark, dreary and wet - puddle wet.

The ocean roars from across the street. The recently updated Best Western has a view of the bay from the second floor balcony, as we watch the water surrounded by the evergreens of the Pacific Northwest. Blue sky over head is a treat, especially this time of year.

We will visit a village of seventy homes later. There is a sense of community as they have a meeting room, library, gym and pool facility amid the newly built community a five minute walk to the ocean. Many of the lots have ocean, bay or forest views.

Later we will shop the outlet stores; perhaps they have even better deals as this recession wears on. Still people complain about the shower head being too high, the bathroom door too close to the toilet. Some things never quite work out for people. Then they add, "It's the best hotel stay we've had in awhile." Sunshine amid the downpours.

My daughter wants to know the difference between a house and a home. I explain people make the difference. She replies a home is a place for family; a house - a thing. She has the essence of what makes a house home. Locally there are many homes for sale, the idea special family moments await inside, inside these beach houses.

The kids have been off school three weeks, an additional week due to snow. Yesterday we drove to the beach after being housebound due to snow and ice. Now flooding closes many roads leading to and from the beach, luckily our route Highway 22 through Salem remains open.

The sun now clears the mountains on the horizon. A beautiful fifty degrees at the coast, warm relative to most of the country. A seagull sounds in the distance. Traffic goes by, yet it is not busy at the beach this time of year. A flag flaps in the wind. A cement truck passes by, then the sound of the surf resumes.

The sun bright in the early morning, the sun refreshing after several weeks of record snow. Perhaps 2009 will bring wondrous things; all is welcome after this past year. The traffic continues a parking lot away, once it passes, the roar of the ocean returns.

The blue sky now fills with cumulus clouds, the sun still bright through the puffy cloud cover. A breeze cools my feet as the sun seeps in through the balcony metal slats. Another seagull passes by, and then returns circling the hotel parking lot. He is joined by yet another seagull as they land atop the hotel sign which greets guests at the street entrance. It's a perch visible only for seagulls along the central Oregon coast.

We write of the sun warming up our morning, drying the pavement and the puddles scattered in hotel parking lots. We note the seagulls, the traffic and the shadows of the metal grating which keeps us safe two floors up.

Just now someone with a rainbow colored shirt places two coffees atop his Volkswagen Bug. He unlocks the trunk and places them in there, and then he pulls out a thermos and transfers the hotel coffee into the larger container. Another hotel guest backs out from their parking space on to their day at the beach.

The sun watches from overhead. I sit so the south wall keeps some sun at bay; otherwise it is too bright without sunglasses.

The traffic lightens up and the surf is once again audible. The bay glistens in the morning sunlight.

The seagulls have since left their perch; they too have a day at the beach ahead of them. We had breakfast earlier, and then the kids wanted one more swim in the hotel pool. I joined them the night before, it was a cold pool. A change of pace for the end of the Christmas break and the start of a new year. 2009, the best is yet to come, with or without the casino shuttle bus. In Las Vegas it was can't miss purple, although the driver had apparently misplaced his clock.

There is a light snow covering the daily paper in our driveway. The beach had its usual variety of weather - downpour, heavy rain, cloudy skies amid early morning sun breaks. We toured a house in the northwest end of town before leaving.

A thirty year old two bedroom, one and a half bath home with a decent ocean view. "There are people sleeping!" the realtor gasps as she quickly backs away and closes the downstairs bedroom door. Later she asks the person at the top of the stairs if maybe we can see the living area only.

The realtor called in advance, yet there is miscommunication. Still we see the common areas inside the small older beach house with its deck overlooking the Pacific Ocean. Neat house, yet not our ideal place at the beach, not home, not just yet.

Later we drive through a new subdivision of seventy planned homes. Some they call estate homes, others mere cottages surround a pool, exercise area and meeting room. The pool has a wave mechanism and there is also a library within the oversized building lobby. In the distance to the south is Siletz Bay; to the west is the Pacific Ocean. Some homes see both bodies of water. Even evergreen forest lines the eastern view. Some smaller cottages might settle for this view alone.

An ocean view beach house might be on many of our wish lists. One day we hope to move in and enjoy time at the coast, days at the beach, rather than yard and house maintenance. We shop the outlet stores and have a late lunch at the casino. Lincoln

City has grown up with its roster of major acts coming to town. Many of the artists enjoy their day at the Oregon coast. We drove through heavy rain, two hours of heavy rain traveling to the coast. We drive through puddles on the return, puddles which slow traffic to ten miles per hour. On the side of the road are overflowing streams and waterfalls in places. Many trees are broken mid trunk due to the recent snow and ice storm. Wood and water, sometimes a deadly combination. Still the day at the coast provides time in the sun atop the hotel room deck, the bay visible in the distance, as seagulls fly about the hotel property.

We return home amid heavy traffic. Happy Valley is covered in a layer of snow. Black ice starts to form as the temperature hovers near freezing. A surprise to see the covering of white after milder weather at the beach. All agree it seems we were away much longer than an overnight. It is always refreshing to get away from routine. A day at the beach works for most of us. The lucky ones spend all their days at the beach.

A layer of ice covers the street. Yesterday's mail had the start of the year end paperwork: a summary rental schedule, a straggling Christmas card from a friend who'd spent the early part of the holiday vacationing with family in Hamburg, Germany. We had spent time in a lunch room on breaks from our banking jobs twenty five years ago in New York City. He is still there, although with another bank, a bank which pays well enough to afford trips abroad. My friend travels often.

He reads a lot. He is interested in reading my book, the one I had e-mailed about, a year ago. The one I said centered on people who leave us early on. They never truly depart as they are with us, beside us as we go on with life. They sit watching as we fill in our everyday, whether working in a bank, doing crossword puzzles in the lunchroom or writing books.

We write of our everyday and those people who people our lives. We mention the business correspondence in our mailbox, and those late greeting cards. We notice the tax forms and the other year end correspondence received annually to remind us a year once again ends. Time to pay for services rendered, even the governments, state and federal, have their familiar reminder tax forms and schedules in the first few days of the new year's mail.

The holiday gift boxes wait in the garage blue bin, ready for next week's recycle schedule. The Christmas tree is back in the garage, stored for another year. The decorations are down, opening up the house. A time to rearrange the furniture, rid of discards. A time of year for renewal, to recommit to not only set goals, and maybe to target results instead.

Even if we don't succeed, hit the bull's eye, we are still moving in the direction. Leaning in the direction we hope to go, be that: physical fitness, financial freedom, reading a bit more often or a wider selection of what we might normally read.

Writing allows us to rethink how our days are going, not just at the start of the new year, rather each day as we sit and write of our moments. The holiday decorations are back in storage, still there are reminders everywhere Christmas has been here once again.

More pictures, cards and mementos find their way on our desks. The new amid the all too familiar. It adds a new layer to our surroundings, finding its way into our writing. Some of it ready for the outgoing mail slot once the layer of ice melts.

School is back in session after the winter break. An old routine begins anew. Abby changes shoes this morning, remembering she has physical education class. She has her books and lunch in her new school bag, an over the shoulder bag from Aeropostale. "It's in style," she tells me.

Madeline wonders if her hair is ok, she finds it fuller this morning. I clear out some of the recyclables after driving the car back in the garage once the kids are driven to school. The recyclables lead to clearing away some garbage from the holiday backlog. Thoughts of Goodwill cross my mind; I should drop off a carload there too. A time of year to rearrange furniture, if not priorities. Less stuff is always a good start.

We unwrap calendars this time of year. We forgo looking at dogs; instead there are calendars of lighthouses, moons, orchids and tropical scenes. Last night's snow is now melted. Rain, heavy rain for much of the night melts the two inches which fell late last night. I wonder if they might have to cancel school, already the kids lost one week due to weather.

We write of our routine, changing schedules, and plans which begin anew with the new year. We clear out our space, we write clearing our thoughts, aligning our priorities. Writing is always at the top of the list, while traveling, or amid the daily routine. It gives order, predictability to our day and often starts our day. We think of the prior day's events, plan for those to come and reflect on the moment at hand.

In front and beside us reminders of the season past. Calendars, cards, photographs and yet to be mailed thank you cards line my desk. The polar bear on one of the Christmas cards watches from the edge of my desk, he lays on his patch of snow. It's almost as though he smiles, his eyes glisten.

The last few days before beginning our new year routine. Madeline gives me a calendar to fit inside my wallet, the day before a tall Harry and David mug. Their food pyramid, Christmas box was finally delivered over the weekend - New Years Eve.

Melissa took the box to work for a coworker's Christmas present. Delayed, yet the weather caused the delay. The weather and the delivery service claimed the mail order vendor. An effective way to distance themselves from their customer, not the most effective way to stay in business long term. They too have a laundry list of things to attend at the start of the new year.

The last of the Christmas letters trickle in. Some manage to fit in more in their year, more people, places and events. Others are on trips abroad visiting family, friends or touring new locations and attend to the yearly card mailing once they return home early January.

We spent an overnight at the beach, once the weather calmed down. Instead of snow and ice, we deal with flooding.

The roadway barely passable in three places due to flooding, the puddles slow us down. Other roads leading inland from the coast are closed. Living along the Oregon coast people accept they will be stranded from time to time. Isolated, and not just on those days of stormy weather.

Still with the computer and cell phones it is harder to truly be isolated. Today service abroad is no longer a year assignment devoid of technology. Not so many years ago those in the service overseas, were serving overseas and they would relate their experience once they return. Today communication is merely altered and not shut off completely.

The second day of school after the Christmas break starts slow. The kids were up late last night, Madeline in the middle of sixth grade science projects. She checks whether our toilets leak. Later tests how much our shower head spills out per minute. She came home with a kit which includes energy efficient light bulbs and a replacement shower head.

Never too early to learn conservation. She also has a neat four by five inch placard noting how much energy we use per appliance. An interesting manual chart of everyday expenses. Most adults have no idea how much energy is used per hour by a television, clothes dryer or other household appliance.

Water and electricity, two commodities which pay to conserve. Meanwhile Abby helps me sort through oceanfront pictures on my den wall. Some look out on the ocean, others look back toward the shore. It is fun receiving her third grade perspective on a wall of photographs.

"The bottom row works well," she says. " It's like they cut the pictures apart." That is the effect we are after. Not so sure we succeed with the top row of six reused calendar page photographs. Calendars are indispensable, even for covering our walls.

The blues, greens and sand of the ocean views are calming. Calming as we start the new year, a new year with its share of new targets. Read we should leave goals by the wayside. Targets, even if not hitting the bull's eye, move us in the right direction. Life a series of small steps into our future, into our destiny. Grace helps us lean into it.

We take it a day at a time, writing a page or three. Sometimes breaking to help with sixth grade science projects, other times adjusting wall photographs with our eight year olds. Still other times pausing to enjoy someone else's past year of activity. A full year of activity from someone now cross country, even though they once lived an apartment away as we shared the everyday on campus.

The darkness outside slowly becomes light. Wind gusts kept us up throughout the night. With each passing day of measurable rain, many are light sleepers. The ground is saturated, two weeks of snow, now rain daily. There have been road closures and landslides. Luckily our trip to the beach was via the road which remains open during this latest wintry weather.

Chapter 31

A vehicle passes along the loop, a neighbor off to work. The kids sleep in a final few minutes before rushing through breakfast, dressing and searching for their backpacks and lunches. Today, I volunteer in third grade.

We sit outside the classroom and read. A group of five or six students alternate reading, then we discuss what was read. The plot, the new words, the main ideas which write the author's story.

Each week I meet these students. They are classmates of my daughter Abby. In essence I've already met them through her. She knows her table of four best, still there is time for socializing at lunch, recess and moving from one learning corner to the next. We read on Wednesday mornings with the hope they read whenever they get a chance.

Reading a skill improved in third grade and used lifelong. Still television competes for their time. Television - watching someone else live.

Television changed the world in the 1950's, similar to the computer revolution. Still the computer is more interactive and essential to everyday life as we know it early 2009. We e-mail, google, and read the daily paper from the computer screen. It's all at our fingertips, if we know where to look, and the machine cooperates.

My old Apple computer was replaced by a used model. Three years now it's ran my spreadsheets and recorded a story or three.

Two days ago one of the programs did not run. It was a tax schedule for 2008.

Pages of financial detail would not boot up. The information is recorded elsewhere, yet requires hours of data entry. Sometimes the computer doesn't cooperate. Suppose this is one of the perks of television it works every time. Whether there is anything worth watching is another matter?

One channel mid afternoon has us living our best life. Another later in the evening has folks weigh in as we watch. Granted sixty percent of America is overweight, still I have trouble finding the merits of observing the weigh in.

Perhaps it changes lives, nonetheless. My daughter later remarked, "We still have to do the exercise for ourselves." I had her repeat her insight. We in fact must live our own lives, not so much watching others live from across a television screen.

A month of weather: snow, ice, and landslides. Today it's mid fifty degrees and windy. Last night's wind left garbage scattered throughout the neighborhood. The daily paper has not been daily this week, or even this month. Interstate 5 between Seattle and Portland is once again closed. This doesn't happen. Recently it's happened twice. Landslides and floods stop the flow of the main interstate system in the western United States.

The wind continues with its occasional gusts. The trees sway, the house rattles. The windows, the fireplace all echo from excess wind. The winter weather returns to this part of the country. My sister sent an attachment on her last e-mail; it is a story of Vermont's latest technology keeping winter roads passable. Apparently more regions of the country struggle through this winter, the weather changed, the budgets strained.

Instead of reading with third grade students in our regular group of five or six, I put together a few packets, six sheets per packet, stapled twice on top. This lasts fifteen minutes, and then I help rewrite their Christmas letters. One runs downstairs only to be told, "Return upstairs and brush your teeth." Later the Christmas letter says what everyone receives: jeans for dad, jewelry for mom, a Rubik's cube for one child, and clothes for the other.

I tell the third grade child her Christmas morning sounds much like ours. She says they could barely sleep the night before. Another child writes of sea turtles. I ask if it is at the Oregon coast. He says they had seen those turtles while in Mexico. His Christmas letter's rough draft is rough. He has more erasure marks and penciled corrections before returning to write it in neat handwriting. He admits early on he has trouble spelling. Still as a third grade student, his Christmas letter holds our interest.

Another writes of her eight days in Cabo San Lucas, Mexico where she swims in the pool and has her hair braided on the beach. She also goes horseback riding. Horseback riding being one word she offers. Also she went riding twice. Later, she adds she went parasailing. Before leaving the classroom, I mention to the teacher this particular student had more fun during Christmas break than the rest of us.

Writing in third grade of our everyday, the routine and the not so routine Christmas vacation. The grade school tourist to Mexico isn't sure where she had a stopover, she thinks maybe Texas. Travel opens our world regardless when or where we travel. Many of us begin traveling much later than third grade. Suppose we begin writing much later too. Years later when we write daily, even amid the unusual high winds and wintry mix of weather this past month delivers.

Interstate 5, the main north south route for the western United States, remains closed. The busiest highway in the west will remain closed several days due to flooding. A main route from Mexico to Canada impassable.

The early new year routine is on. Many attempt to control their weight, finances - life. Television and magazines capitalize on this time of year. Meanwhile retailers continue to struggle, some closing their doors, or cutting back on their number of stores. A segment continues to grow while others close down.

Today it is nine Macy's stores being shuttered. The other day William Sonoma was mentioned.

People aren't spending as freely. Yesterday we were reminded we caused the economic mess. Us, those of us who saved for the future. The message stings, the implication we are careless. Still to reprimand the average upper middle class person is shortsighted. This segment of the population has all but disappeared. Today, we are headed where one is either rich or not so much.

The United States not immune to the economic reality of much of the world. There is trouble in the distribution system, not merely a problem with our main western United States highway. The redistribution, allocation of resources is a global problem. Even the folks amid the most prosperous country on earth can't get it right. We can't keep the channels open, our roadways clogged, even closed.

We write of the heat kicking on, the traffic outside, and the economic malaise. We note the shadow of our writing hand, and those events and circumstances which shadow our life. Like a gust of wind they are there. Like a neighbor who pulls away quickly as they rush off to work. Writing takes the time to notice and log in the everyday.

We write what happens to us and those around us. We mention what is atop our desk and boxed next to our desk. I spent part of yesterday boxing up twenty books ready for Goodwill. Time for someone else to enjoy reading those books. One never knows what a book will reveal, those we recycle and even those we pencil in ourselves. I also threw out old utility bills and paperwork from years earlier.

We hang on to stuff which once was important. Years later it's apt to be less important. Some books we keep, knowing we will browse through them once again. Others get tossed in the nearby box waiting to be carted away.

Early in the new year people make resolutions. Early on those resolutions bend to accommodate the everyday. Writing down our intentions move them closer to reality. It's no different than writing our books: one word, one morning, one new year at a time. Taking time to recycle stuff which no longer fits our life, or den space. We recycle ongoing, more so at the start of a new year.

There is more desktop this morning. There is also more space in the desk drawer and bookshelves. Always a good feeling when we remove the clutter, especially within our work space. It gives us more room to write, and more room to write within. It clears our physical space as well as space in our lives.

We now see the photographs on our desk. We see the pictures on the surrounding wall. Rather than a mishmash of correspondence, there is now a clear pile of books, a pile of papers and the free space within which we write.

Our neighbor lost a section of her fence from the windstorm two days ago. Debris is scattered about the neighborhood as the storm coincides with garbage day. Fortunately the recycle crew made it through last week after missing two weeks due to wintry weather. This during the holiday season which generates even more heaps for them to collect.

One of the exciting things of clearing our space is finding things we've long misplaced or forgotten. The garage bookshelves yield a book I read while on a bus tour of Europe in the summer of 1984. My seat companion for part of the tour read it and left it behind.

Midweek started off on a late and hectic schedule. We leave without wallet and keys. The car and house keys remain in my desk drawer. We stand in the car garage - one of those days.

I take the garage door opener with me as we walk to school. The kids slept late and thus our midweek routine started late and never caught up until we are locked outside the house. At school we read a few more Christmas stories of how vacation was spent.

Two third grade students write of vacations in Mexico, another of their early morning Christmas and the gifts received. My daughter writes her page long story along a similar vein.

Later I walk back home and read in the car, in the garage in the car. Luckily there are bookcases down there. I pick up several books to fill the midmorning until late afternoon timeframe. One book is on taking risks, the one my friend from the tour gave me twenty five years ago. It is fun to recollect my tour mates, the tour itself and how reading a book years later we wonder how its words were understood all those years before. Long before life allows us to live twice as many pages.

Later I walk back to school and pick up my daughters. They play ball and do a bit of homework as we wait for my wife to come home with her house key. She runs late and thus it is a full day of sitting in the garage reading. "It's really not that bad living in a car," says my youngest daughter.

We point out those who live in a car don't have the garage or house to go along with that car. Suddenly she better understands the plight of someone living out of their vehicle. Still it requires they be resourceful enough to adapt to living in a small space and limit their worldly possessions.

Too many accumulate on going. We no longer see the desk in front of us. Some days we leave behind our keys which can reveal a day unlike any other. We adjust our routine which is the definition of risk itself.

A train whistle awakes us this morning. The sound alone among the early morning quiet. Yesterday my computer crashed for the last time. My original computer broke down three years ago. I'd bought a similar one and used it for several years. Lately it has been temperamental and never sure I can rely on it. Often turning it off and then back on restarts the program, printer or troublesome computer itself.

I spent most of yesterday updating several pages of spreadsheet for tax purposes. It took awhile to program it and then enter the data. I've used a similar format for over fifteen years, adjusting the numerical details as needed.

My youngest daughter wonders why I spend time at the end of each year recording numbers. "Aren't they already there?" she asks. She thinks the numbers remain the same year in and year out. I explain they not only change, ideally they grow larger with the passage of time. 2008 is an exception, an exception many of us learn as the year progressed. Still others will get a better appreciation of how ugly 2008 was financially speaking as they organize their records.

There is no good news at year end.

Even my computer struggles to print out the data; it too doesn't want to see those figures. The printer prints out documents which lack color, rather than the vibrant pie charts of years past. This year it is a grayish series of lines to delineate the pie sections. It's a blur, the details read better that way this year.

One bank year end summary has a footnote we have six months only to question or even sue over the bank statement figures. In between the lines, one could assume the bank knows ahead of time customers won't feel grateful as to how the bank invested their funds. The investment staff is no better than the guy on the street, both lost, major losses this bank hopes to appease by its footnote.

A train whistle wakes us up. Early morning and all is quiet other than an occasional wind gust. Last week's storm closed a section of Interstate 5. Our neighbor lost a section of her fence. Maybe the winter storm adds to the computer troubles. Still it is time for replacement as it is no longer time or cost effective to trust in a temperamental computer.

Sometimes it reveals the numbers, the data hours spent inputting, other times the document won't open. Many wish 2008 had locked up early on. We will upgrade the computer and hope for the best in 2009. Realistically our numbers will grow as the new year unfolds.

The shadow of my writing hand continues to move across the page as the kids pour their early morning cereal. A mix of cereal bowl moving across the kitchen counter and plastic wrap being stored in the cupboard below. Just now the coffee pot beeps to signal the brew is ready. The three pages are barely begun this morning, another late start to a mid January day. My oldest daughter asks Abby to step up the morning pace.

A surprise this morning as Madeline drops off a coffee mug with hot coffee on my desk. It is an oversized mug she gave me this Christmas. This particular Harry and David delivery made it on time. The food pyramid, not so much, gets here for New Years. The coffee is hot as I take a sip. The kids pour a bit more cereal in their breakfast bowls.

Mid forty degrees this morning and perhaps we will resume our regular winter weather. Many still ask what the past month of wintry snow and ice were all about, while others suffer the effects of flooding. We write of our day and what happens throughout our days. Today a list is on my desk, some items already crossed off, others weeks behind. I will make the car appointment and hope they can change the oil this week.

Goodwill is also on my list. The time of year to clear out our space, clear out our excess accumulation from last year and the years before. Making room for change, allows new opportunities into our lives.

Initially we jot down what we want to happen and sooner or later we drive to Goodwill or the auto repair shop. Writing it down makes it happen. Even writing progresses one word at a time. Our hand's shadow moves across the page, and eventually words fill in the story. Later often months later, we reread to see what we wrote, what the words have to say? How the story comes together after spending months logging in our time.

Chapter 32

Linda wants to know how we enjoyed the recent bestseller she introduced during our weekly Bible study. Most agree it brings up valid questions about life, death, and God. It touched us, each in our own way. Books do this. We read them from our own perspective, from our own life of experience. Books, plots and people met within story. Imagine how live people affect us day to day even those left behind years before. Those introduced among our book's details, the things we tell strangers.

Whether visiting in a Tenderloin residential hotel lobby, abducted at an Oregon lake campsite, or drowning beneath a load of logs in a Vermont millpond doesn't matter, those are mere details which add to narrative.

The essence of those stories, some dark and tragic, is what happens in spite of those days of anguish. We go forward, forever changed. The lucky realize we take them along like a book which resonates, long after returning it to the bookshelf.

People too are introduced and recognized by the books they introduce and recommend to others. Books do this whether we merely pass along a favorite, a bestseller or write one of our own. Sometimes it seems others have written our book, as we read along. Other times, we read our book as we write along.

Too often it is a painful recognition of details which changed our life long ago. Sometimes this is an abrupt way to meet people, especially when they recommend a book without their knowing it is in many respects a story we could write.

We lived many of those same details; we relive them as we turn pages thirty through fifty as it were. Those passages define life; they make us who we are. Regardless what work we choose to do, we do it differently that day and each day going forward with a special someone at our side - a sibling within.

Chapter 33

⎯⎯•◈•⎯⎯

We write to clear our minds, to get our thoughts on the page. Often later we realize we merely hold the pen, words written through us, not so much from us. We write amid the children's chatter in the early morning breakfast. We listen in to ourselves or others in rooms away. My youngest tries her best to stay home from school. The tears spill over as she tells my older daughter her worries.

"Let me ask real quick," says Madeline, inferring she will request her younger sister stay home from school. Abby stays home. Her tummy ache is better by noon. We spend the day moving furniture. She gets the older computer rewired into her new Christmas desk. Before moving the wires we spend time looking through old e-mails, some ten years old.

There is the back and forth note, e-mail of someone leaving us via the sometimes slow process of cancer. There are the excited e-mails of my daughter's birth, first tooth, and first steps. It is fun to recollect those moments eight years earlier.

The computer the same, otherwise the home, people and time have moved on. It is fun having my third grade daughter read through the e-mails, only later does she realize we read about her birth, tooth and first steps. Reading of ourselves is always a surprise, even if we write down those words. She reads further on how life was spent eight years earlier.

Later we have her personal computer set up in her bedroom bookcase. I take the computer cart on rollers and place it in my den, getting rid of the much bulkier L shaped desk which overtook my den space for a few years. The laptop is wired online. My Apple computer is used offline only, lately it has been temperamental. I move it to its new space atop the portable cart. I hope soon there will be a more updated Apple model sitting there, one I can rely on whenever I boot up the machine.

Still it will require programming new schedules and spreadsheets. Sometimes it's good to start anew. Other days it's equally fun reading about life ten years earlier, the days in our first home, having children, and spending time with my mother in law. She spent three months of the year with us. The good old days, before visiting Wallowa Lake.

Later my daughter practices her typing using a school purchased keyboarding tutorial. She can't wait to show her older sister the progress we made in rearranging furniture. Now my oldest daughter has more room in her bedroom. Soon she will get a laptop of her own, one she has been wishing for, for a long time.

Today I'll drive downtown for an oil change. I hope it's quick enough to allow time to drop off the oversized computer desk at a consignment store, the same store where I found the desk years before. I also bought the matching file cabinet and bookcases.

There is a light wind outside. Seems balmy after weeks of winter weather, now the storms move east. Madeline has a school report on weather tomorrow. She starts the report with, "This is Meteorologist Madeline in the Morning." She has a map of the differing weather patterns across the United States. She explains the various fronts and how they affect weather, create weather.

Abby and I read a National Geographic booklet on weather as we wait in the car across the street from the school. I read to Abby as she looks through the rear window watching for her sister. She is too excited about her new room arrangement to focus on weather patterns. Her tummy ache long gone, she has a memorable day off from school, going back to the beginning of her story, literally recognizing herself in the words.

Sometimes it is good to upgrade, other times it is necessary not only to maintain yet rather toss aside the old and go with new. Like the weather changes, our lives are in a constant state of flux. Some days the degree of change is more noticeable.

The coffee beeps from the kitchen. The kids toss in bed. Today, Meteorologist Madeline in the Morning on KNYK has a weather report to give to her sixth grade class. The call letters stand for Now You Know. She is excited to show her United States map covered with all things weather related.

"Dad your coffee!" Madeline yells from the kitchen as Abby sleeps in awhile longer. I'll be in Abby's third grade classroom later at nine this morning to volunteer. Usually we separate in small reading groups. Some days the hour on a story of their own, journaling in grade school. The weather has calmed down outside, nice to wear sweaters only mid winter.

Last night the Bible study group emphasized the spread of the Catholic Church and the road blocks encountered. All agree life hasn't changed much in two thousand years. Clearly there are technological advances along with improvements in medicine, yet human nature remains the same.

Even with the advancements of two thousand years, man still resists change. It takes a miracle for some to see the light. Doubt still blocking faith in building community. The discussion veers several times, once noting a local author's bestseller.

Another time noting there is a book series titled The Bible For. There is one for housewives, school teachers, and plumbers etcetera. I thought no harm done if it opens a conversation, specifically one centered on the Bible, God and his word. Others find it disrespectful, sacrilegious. There is only one Bible, no sequels or editing allowed. Wonder how God feels about this? Assuming those folks don't believe they rewrite the actual Bible.

Still moving our books off the store bookshelves not only requires clever wording, an equally clever title catches the reading audience's attention in the first place. Thus say the bibles on writing, the books which help us word our pages. Those words which carry a story within and often let us read more of the human condition.

After rearranging the home office there is less writing space, my desk has shrunk. It opens up the space in the den. This new configuration looks better; still it will take time adjusting to the new layout.

Just now I notice the printer case is open. My daughter Madeline must have printed her weather report fact sheet on it. She eats breakfast as Abby squeezes in a few more minutes of sleep time. They were up late watching television. A new season of American Idol. They are in Phoenix, one of our favorite places to vacation.

A quick flight from Portland, the sun filled area is an enticing and reasonably priced vacation spot. There is food, shopping and of course the sun drenched pools. We've had several memorable vacations there. It's where Abby learns to swim.

The weather should not dictate vacations or even party memories. Still it often does color the day and event. We abide by what goes on outside and whether we will spend time outdoors. Most aren't spending their days outside in Portland mid winter. Still having to wear only the extra layer of a sweater is welcomed. I hope Madeline's later weather report is well received by her sixth grade classmates, and Mrs. Onstott.

Wednesday morning is spent volunteering in my daughter Abigail's third grade classroom. First I stapled the food pyramid projects to the hallway bulletin board, outside the classroom door. Earlier I visited with my friend Marilyn who also volunteers Wednesday mornings.

She wonders how my meeting went with a local author. She also wants to know how last week ended. I had locked myself out of the house the last time we met. I tell her I spent the day in the car, in the garage in the car - reading.

As for the author meeting, it went well. She warned to not expect financial rewards early on. Write for the love of writing, for the art of writing itself. Also she too had people who were less than enthusiastic about her writing venture. Write nonetheless, in spite of them, in spite of ourselves. Write what wants to get written. Take the time, make time to get our thoughts, ideas on the page.

Sooner or later we will have a book sitting in front of us. Whether it sells is not the main reason people write. We write for ourselves first and foremost. Maybe even for those who left long ago and watch from nearby. Just maybe we help finish writing their book, telling their story.

Marilyn listened. She was encouraging, even though we both know life is what we make of it. In other words, some go for it, in spite of knowing the drill, the complications. Still others venture forward not quite knowing all the potential pitfalls.

Later in the classroom we read the book, F - Is for Freedom. A story involving Amanda and her family who put up Hannah's family as they move along the Underground Railroad. One third grade student remarks she is familiar with subways. It's a start and I hope she has a better understanding, appreciation for the Underground Railroad after we read the first two chapters of F - Is for Freedom.

Another group of five third grade students read of the San Francisco earthquake. In 1906 San Francisco was the largest west coast city. We read about the rattling, rolling, and rumbling of the thunder beneath the ground.

An earthquake takes us by surprise, often moving us further along our journey. They had all been to California and had their own experiences with earthquakes. I tell them I was in the 1989 San Francisco earthquake, and is the reason I live in Portland. Decades later and it allows me to read with them this morning in their third grade classroom.

Wednesdays are a break in an otherwise routine week. Yesterday my daughter asked why I stayed in the class so long. I spent an additional hour helping another group read. Before leaving the classroom, I leave with Abby as she breaks down crying her throat hurts. Apparently her condition travels!

She is asleep within minutes of getting home. Later she fills in world flags on a recent school homework project. She colors in the flags as I search Craigslist for office furniture and a new computer. The afternoon passes quickly and then it is time to pick up Madeline. She is elated to have her oral report on weather done. Another midweek day doesn't go quite as planned and yet reveals much to write about.

We hear different things, thus no two stories are the same, even those written down. This morning it is barely twenty nine degrees outside. Seems cold after a few days of unseasonably warm weather. My computer is back up running.

I spent part of yesterday waiting for someone to call; they had a computer to sell. By noon I e-mail I am no longer interested. No longer interested in the computer, printer and whatever else they might throw in the deal. Instead I wait for a telephone call the entire morning and another telephone call promised the night before.

Part of life is showing up, doing what we say we will do. "Maybe he misunderstood what he said?" my daughter remarks. A lesson there among the loss. Not only did we not get a new computer, the seller lost a customer. Maybe they have another buyer on telephone hold?

The furnace blows warm air into the room; it will run for much of today. Abby sleeps in. She had a stomach ache, then sore throat, now just under the weather. Her table of four at school had a similar time of it weeks earlier. One went to the doctor and was told there was no prescription needed. Time will get him back to normal. Time heals, so too for writing - it hears us.

Sometimes we write what we hear from our everyday. Taking note of the telephone calls which don't come through, the overheard comments throughout the day and even those insights from a third grade child. Perhaps he didn't understand what he said, not the most efficient way to run a business, let alone life.

Writing is a time to collect our thoughts, and jot down those which cross our mind. The furnace fills the room with heat;

much like a plot, it fills the pages, it writes our books. We only have to pause long enough to recognize the story. Often it writes itself if only we step aside.

A few extra pancakes wait in the kitchen; I hope Abby wakes us before the clock's morning is over. She has kept busy with her computer, stuffed animals and reading more Judy Moody. Her reading improves. All skills improve with practice, even writing, and the listening behind writing.

We write of what is on our desks and what we hope would be on our desks a day later. Instead the old computer stares from its own computer cart. It will boot up a few more times.

Chapter 34

A new year begins. We log in all things financial from the previous year, which makes tax time less of a hassle. It also previews the year ahead, and I hope better times are ahead. Writing allows time between the future plans and past recollections.

It forces us to spend time in the present moment, which is a gift in itself, a present. The present is all there is. In the meantime we listen for something to write.

Abby was again under the weather so we spent yesterday together. Early on she was hungry. The breakfast pancakes didn't hold her until lunch. Still we ate a late lunch of tuna sandwiches as I wanted to finish up with computer work.

2008 is now over, so is much of the paperwork which goes along with closing up a year. Seeing the numbers written down brings the point home. Many no doubt have similar reactions: seeing their accounts down, their income down, and where they stand at this year's end.

Today there is frost on the roofs. A long weekend with no one out and about. Inside the kids sleep in the family room after a family slumber party. They watched television late into the night on this the start of a three day weekend. They also read a bit with their portable lights attached to their books. Whatever furthers their reading is a good thing.

Madeline receives a "Wow!" from her teacher. A recent test got the ire of the teacher as few students passed her test. Madeline did well and receives the written "Wow!" from Mrs. Onstott. It too is a good thing.

Two days ago there was an advertisement on Craigslist for an editor. Someone had written a memoir and wanted someone else to edit. It had been edited many times; still it needed more, perhaps less. I respond much writing is biographical and perhaps we could meet to discuss her work. Work begun because someone had said "Wow! You could write a book. You should write a book." It happens.

Many hear that line or even use it. Each of us has a story to tell. A memoir is a slice of time in our life. An autobiography on the other hand, is a one time write up of our entire life. It's two days later and I haven't heard from the person on Craigslist with the memoir to rewrite, edit. Sharing our words with others is always a risk, more so for those we place in our writing, or write because of their place in our lives.

Some live to write, others prefer to sit outside the storyline. A memoir captures a moment in our lives. My first thought was she might be writing of a time spent away, a new friendship, a new culture, perhaps a new language, maybe serving overseas in some capacity. Then again it might be a more personal story of struggle within a familiar family setting. Either way her memoir backdrop pushes others to the point of saying "Wow! You should write this down."

Editing is the next step after months of writing stuff down, laying track as the books on writing refer to it. Editing lets us go back and read the story as though for the first time. It is. We are the story's first reader only once we review what we have written do we find the thread of a story within. We find where it leads and add here and take from there to give it clearer direction.

Writing builds with each rewrite. True whether we are the ones editing our own words or have a complete stranger read through our memoirs. Either way a story gets better, not the actual story, rather in how it is told. How it is written and ultimately heard by future readers. Let's hope it fills them between reads.

We write in the early morning quiet. There is an occasional gust of wind to distract. Yesterday they were louder and more frequent. Late afternoon the power went out for forty five minutes. A windy winter in the Pacific Northwest. A colder winter for much of the nation, even parts not usually associated with winter's cold. A car shifts in the distance. Few are on the road this early, early Sunday morning. Last night a stretch limousine dropped by to hoist a neighbor away for a late fortieth birthday party. She left with her boyfriend, sister and cousin to celebrate the turning of a new decade.

The calendar already two weeks into it's new year. Yesterday we delivered a calendar to a friend, a belated Christmas gift. The orchid calendar is a final present among the rest of food gift items. Just now the lights flicker. They did throughout yesterday, and then finally the electricity was gone. Short of cell phones, there were no telephone calls.

I spent part of the afternoon on line reviewing Craigslist postings. This year more people recycle their furniture, computer equipment and any other item which has outlived its usefulness. A new year and people want a fresh start.

Often it means more than simply rearranging things, they want replacement. Even new used works. "New, used," a neighbor once said about his 1965 Lincoln Continental. It was the model with the reverse rear doors, suicide doors some called them.

I noticed his car, a white classic Lincoln. He later told me it was new for him, although he bought it used. He still lives in the same apartment more than twenty years later. Wonder if the white Lincoln is in the garage. He had used the attached garage for years and refused to give it up once I bought the three apartment building. He got his way and remains a tenant even today. The situation works for me and it's been a comfortable home, accommodation for him.

We've moved several times since. He stays put within the same apartment all these years later. The other day I saw him with an electric wheelchair going down the sidewalk. Wonder if he is still able to drive? Perhaps his white Lincoln will be posted on Craigslist too, maybe it already has. There are pages of new postings daily. Amazing, when we consider this is just scanning the Portland metropolitan area.

Thus there are exponentially more postings in any one day. It fills a day browsing, window shopping from our home personal computers. Inside warm, while the outside stirs anything not tied down or heavy, even electricity has trouble staying in place.

We write in the early morning calm. We write about the calm and the wind which blows through our day. We notice what took part of recent days. The weather, the Craigslist postings, the ongoing writing. Writing fills our everyday, even those filled with wind gusts, white Lincolns and stretch limousines.

The wind howls outside, another cold start to a mid January day. Each day gets a bit longer and warmer, in theory at least. Much of the country has record cold. The coffee brews from the kitchen. Yesterday there was no coffee. A lazy day watching reruns on television. Also a continuing education program on ageism. She suggests children are often treated as kids, she doesn't mean it in a good way. Thus their opinions don't matter, to adults at least.

She mentions things wrong with America, the America which offers her opportunity. A foreigner she ends up attending a top college. Still she is a dynamic presenter as she speaks of how people are resilient. We shut off detractors through laughter, tears, activity and relationship. The chemistry of sorrow filled tears differs from those tears of joy. Some think it explains the longevity of women, they are more apt to show their emotions, live their emotions. Apparently it is a healthier way to prolong life.

Sunday's message was to see and hear, look and listen. Many of us are distracted. We can't remember the first thing we heard this morning, much less recall our last thought the night before. Having an off day allows us to slow down, to regroup, and to take the time for ourselves. It's our body's way of taking a needed break, catching a breath. Caught up in the busy-ness of everyday time slips away from us, if we allow it to happen.

The coffee is now on my writing desk. The scent of coffee too, is a good thing. The hum of the furnace is at my feet. Clear skies have kept the temperature cold overnight. The washing machine whirls a load of clothes, the two week old dryer waits its turn.

Today is a holiday, a catch up day for many. Others sleep as their everyday doesn't allow this later sleep schedule. I will sort through more stuff for Goodwill. Last week Abby was home for much of the school week. Sometimes having others help sort is not time effective. They are an additional set of memories recollecting sentimental items.

Still it's always a good feeling opening up our space; otherwise our workspaces become crowded, burdened with knick knacks from another time. They anchor us to a spot in time, thus making it more difficult for newness to enter into our lives. We accumulate a day at a time, one shopping trip at a time. America has consumption down.

Not so much production these days. Many industries struggle while others close their door. Our second largest electronics company, Circuit City, closed its doors last week. Even the mail order gourmet foods struggle. They fall behind, as the middle class struggles. They didn't have tens of thousands to lose, maybe hundreds of thousands when we add in home depreciation.

Times are changing; can this downward cycle be at ebb? Many look forward to good times flowing again. January of the new year is almost over. Still the news is not welcomed on most fronts, including the cold front hovering over much of America. The big desk is gone. Today it is back at the consignment shop looking for a new owner, a new office to occupy.

My den is now more open. There is a computer cart nearby holding an older model Apple computer. My laptop wired for online sits on my smaller writing desk. It's a more functional space. Changing or rearranging furniture starts a domino effect. There are still magazines and paperwork to sort through.

Many of the books will soon return to Goodwill so they can circulate. It's often more fun to own our books, so we can jot down ideas within their pages. Some are worth rereading, thus they linger on our bookshelves, even those books with postcards found within.

The desk was a part of a set with file cabinet and bookshelves. The other parts work well enough in my den; the desk on the other hand overpowered the room. A wind stirs outside. Read yesterday a wind can also sough. Hadn't seen this word before, much less knew the wind could sough outside.

Like meeting someone for the first time, we use their name immediately to pronounce it correctly. Then we use it again mid conversation and later when we part company. Thus it imprints the person's name on our memory. Suppose learning a new word is much the same. We use it, use it again and from then on, have it readily available. This morning the wind soughs.

Chapter 35

I spent two weeks at my cousins when my younger sister was born. Sometimes we are asked "What do you plan to do with your life?" As children we haven't a clue, even as adults we aren't always so sure.

Still it's not so much the doing or having that matter in life. Not so much busying ourselves with work, or accumulating, surrounding ourselves with things, rather it is who we become in the process of living life.

Some days will invariably be met with the death of another. A death which gives us reason to live, gives us the what we are going to do with our life. In the meantime, we take those loved ones along. Sometimes we write their story down in books; theirs, ours and we hope parts of yours, the book's second reader.

Over thirty five years ago, before pages thirty through fifty, I was sent to my cousins. In writing we see where we've been, who we meet, and who we become. Being much more important than what we do or plan to do in life. Who we become much more important than what we accumulate as we pass through.

Stories are penciled in on paper in the early morning autumn fog. The decades old character sketches in our desk drawer resurface and tell of how life once was inside the middle. Other times, it is the wave of a child Grace's banner, which catches our attention from across a grade school library.

Still other days a bestseller inadvertently falls in our lap. Like a late model Ford truck parked houses away, it too stops us in our tracks. Only then are we free to move, contrasted with our loss, we celebrate life, ironically enhanced by loss. Our sibling within writes our books and reveals our life alongside theirs.

Chapter 36

————⟨⟩⟨⟩————

The winds of change sough in our nation's capital as we change President today. Every four years we, the people, elect a new leader. We, the people, in theory at least. There are many nuances and levels of electorate; it makes us dizzy, or apathetic. Add the media to the mix, and it is a spectacle. Even on Election Day, we remain a divided country, regardless of the chatter, music and political rhetoric.

Today's newspaper has a scandal on a newly elected mayor. He comments from our nation's capital. This is post election and thus less damaging to political life.

Maybe not, as things change, or so promises the new administration in Washington. Time will tell if they deliver on their campaign promises. They stayed on message during the campaign, even amid the soughing wind.

Recently a friend recommended a book. It was one of those rare books. She promised each of us would read it differently, due to our varied prior experiences. Each of us hears a story differently. Sometimes it resonates with us other times, not so much. This book touches her. It touches the author, although the story is about his friend. The author has a handle on language, as his friend grips his loss, a family loss which ironically adds to his life.

Those of us, who have lost, never forget the experience. We are to keep the lesson amid the loss. A sibling within - what loss gives us. Loss makes us who we are, as much as gain, the wins in life.

Setting pulls in the reader as the author continues with the plot. This book's setting is Oregon which has been home for the second part of my life. It starts in Portland, stops at Multnomah Falls, and Hood River on its way to Wallowa Lake in eastern Oregon.

Setting pulls in a reader, it grasps us like nothing else can. We carry those life defining settings long after we physically leave them behind. In truth we never leave those settings or the people lost in those settings. We take them with us, or maybe more apt, they take us with them. They write our books alongside us. They live life beside us as we move into each new day, even decades later.

Linda has several copies of this recent bestseller she wants to share with her Bible study group. While not strictly a religious book, it touches God, life and Linda. She wants to pass this on to others. The author is from Gresham and we lived there just six years ago for as many years.

Yesterday I spent part of the day running errands in its downtown and drove by our old home. They've since added a second level and a new baby girl as three pink balloons hang outside the front entrance.

I miss the sense of community in Gresham. The library, church, banks and shopping are just steps away rather than a car ride away in our new updated neighborhood. Much of our new community did not exist just five years ago. Granted five years can be long enough for some, give or take a day or two.

Life includes a dose of sad in order to move on to the good, the venturesome. Sometimes friends help move us along, or at a minimum, move their favorite books. They in turn speak to us, although in perhaps not the way the person recommending the book expects.

The recyclables are curbside. My bookshelves steadily unload. Goodwill received fifty books the day before. I left with a new book, sheet music to one of my favorite songs, "Easy" by Lionel

Ritchie. I first heard it blaring from army barracks at Fort Ord, outside Monterey California in the late 1970's.

Easy like Sunday morning goes the song. Yesterday our new President took the oath of office a second time in as many days. Meanwhile the former President and his wife return to Texas. The media reports their net worth is down by a third. Apparently they aren't immune to the recession which lingers.

Last week Circuit City the second largest electronics store shuttered its doors. Today we read Intel considers closing four plants, one on the west side of Portland.

I finish reading the bestseller I was given the night before. While it brings up many issues useful for book clubs, the narrative is dark. I find the best selling book difficult to read. Still it delves into forgiveness and many matters about our thoughts on God, all three persons, God the father, his son Jesus, and the Holy Spirit.

Volunteering in yesterday's third grade class, Moses read more of the Underground Railroad. Later another group read of the Torries and the kid who looked forward to war, uniforms, flags, and camaraderie. Suppose he got one thing right, although most would prefer the end of wars - all war.

The best selling book mentions forgiveness as a strangle hold around someone's neck. Forgiveness is for us and it doesn't necessarily follow that relationships immediately resume. It might happen down the road, still there is a sense of trust, a bond must be rebuilt. The breach in the bond of trust is what severs relationships. Relationships, the living of life knowing we are loved. Many Americans live to accumulate, to consume. We live for things, perhaps in an effort to keep us distant, insulated - and loved.

The author writes of a person who loses a child while on a camping trip. Loss of a child is perhaps one of life's true tragedies. Still loved ones never leave our side. So too for God, whether we are cognizant of his presence or not. He is beside us at every bend in the road. Even those days when our loved ones wave a final goodbye as they round the road's curve. Or more importantly, when they don't return at day's end.

The shadow of my writing hand moves across the page. There is frost this morning. Today Madeline has a violin concert, Abby a state wide math test. We write of what we read and the places we go. Ideally, we write of what we take along, learning as we grow.

Madeline has a test on weather, everything she has learned on the topic since the beginning of the school year. She wonders why they didn't test ongoing. Last night we met on having our third grade children take statewide math tests. The teachers are not concerned with grades at this point.

We, as parents, were given a sample test. It called for answering a math question four different ways. Once by using words, once by numbers, once by pictures and finally a check it section whereby proving the correct answer. Not a bad way of answering any question, let alone third grade math puzzles.

Today Abby has a doctor's appointment. She sings from the kitchen as the dishwasher hums in the background. She has been under the weather for a few weeks now. Her tablemates each have had a similar bug, still she is off to the doctors later today.

A cold day outside, the winter rains have been away for a few weeks and the clear skies keep it cold. The wind adds to the chill. Madeline learns about the various layers above us. How the hole in the ozone isn't such a good thing? What happens when differing air masses meet? What forms clouds, cold fronts and leads to global warming? She studies what a meteorologist does, and what he relies on to make his weather forecasts.

Abby's cereal bowl rattles from the kitchen. An airplane flies by, as a car shifts along the loop. The dishwasher further along in its cycle, as Abby shifts in her bar stool. Another plane climbs in the distant sky, climbing toward our neighborhood as the sound gets louder. We write what goes on indoors, outdoors and from afar. Just now the furnace is back on. It has its work cut out for itself this cold morning.

My Harry and David oversized coffee mug to my left, it's nearly half gone as the gourmet company struggles in this economy. Yesterday I walked through a bookstore; it was a book exchange, resale bookstore. The bookcases were lined with fiction, only two shelves had the "How to do it?" or other nonfiction. The business and biography section were noticeably missing. The owner said he sells what people read. Apparently people keep it real via reality television, or live vicariously through lines of fiction.

Many garage sales later, I learned what people read. The nonfiction ends up at Goodwill. Actually there was a customer who took several of the books, shaking her head not understanding fiction's allure. Still reading books changes lives, even the fiction writers' lives are changed or perhaps revealed as they write along. Readers escape into the author's reality, imagination or a blend of both.

Books take us elsewhere just as in Austria, the music is written in the wind. Regardless of the climate, there is something to sing about daily, write about daily for the writers among us. Ms. Cameron said writers surround us, so too for the stories waiting to be heard and written down. The better stories tell all of our story.

The doctor looks through Abby's chart and finds last year at this time she had a sinus infection. Two weeks later we now know why Abby has been extra sensitive. She doesn't care to go to school and wants to be close by, clinging like a preschooler. It is not Abby; still independence is a desirable trait.

An airplane flies by breaking the early morning quiet. On the political scene our new President finishes his first partial week in office. New York has a new senator. Governor Sarah Palin has a book deal in the works.

CNN reports she will have to give ugly details on the McCains. More accurately she may just tell her story, the whole unvarnished truth, which alone is a bestseller for half of America, those proud to be Americans long before this election cycle. Meanwhile the stock and housing markets continue to plummet.

Another airplane makes its way across the sky. The daily newspaper waits in the driveway. Another cold night as the furnace stays on much longer than usual this morning. We may drive to the beach later, taking advantage of the three day weekend.

Today is my mother's eighty first birthday. Last year there was a surprise party. Across town my next door neighbor, aunt Alice, was saying a final farewell. Sometimes there are too many activities at once, some not planned in advance.

The morning calm is broken by distant traffic. My computer mouse blinks on and off. I will boot up the laptop later to check e-mail and any late breaking news. Much of it reported as late breaking, although we realize it first aired hours earlier.

Another plane makes its way across the early morning sky. My writing pen shadow moves its way across the page. We write in the early morning regardless of our child's diagnosis or the daily media feed. We write in spite of the political rhetoric or scandal.

Chapter 37

Stories are penciled in ongoing, even those written long ago in the early morning fog. The stories found amid a Tenderloin hotel lobby. The stories left behind in a Vermont sawmill pond, or begun there.

Once we have a certain number of character sketches, the story is written, the story writes itself. All that's left is to shuffle the deck of characters and weave them into our story. That is the hard part, where does the story start or even end. Like all good stories, it starts in the middle.

Inside the middle, start there and then return to introduce and later conclude what we have written. Some days it is simple enough, we write what we've read, imagined, or maybe lived which seems fiction at this point, foreign to us, foreign to our life today. Still we must add those characters and include ourselves in the mix to write our books.

Words tell a story, so too for the people in that story; those who write it, those who live it, and those who later come along and read about it. Words and their people tell a story whether in a Tenderloin residential hotel lobby, within family, a group Bible study, or even as we walk through our neighborhood within our own thoughts.

Writing echoes our voice. We use details from our life to write our own story. Sometimes we use details from our life to write the story of others, the story of humanity reflected within those details. All of them, even those twenty pages which ultimately refocus, if not define life.

Many stories hint of God, or an interconnection within our universe. He is there whether we write about him or not. He is reflected in our stories and most likely prefers we include details of his life within the mix.

This writing stirs, moves, it gives voice to perhaps an echo from those who touch us along the way. Even those who once asked us as kids, "What do you plan to do with your life?" We write, so others can read alongside our story and ideally hear more of their own.

Books do this on occasion; the better ones do it every time. We read of ourselves, our life echoed in the detail, voice echoed in the writing, our words echoed in story. Each of us has one, a story filled with laughter, tears, activity and relationship.

Each of us has one, a story or three. We tell them we are working on it, placing words on the page is the least of it. Our book has already been written, now we must get through the words. Varied as the details may be, they make us who we are, and write our books. Rather than a notation on a calendar, they fill our books and tell our story - one setting, one sibling at a time.

We write about it so others can read along and ideally hear more of their own story. Their story, the one which echoes their voice, their life. Perhaps not necessarily the one they had planned for themselves, much less recognize in someone else's words. Still no story is told in its entirety - it's just some echo longer.